RAILWAY HERITAGE
PORTSMOUTH

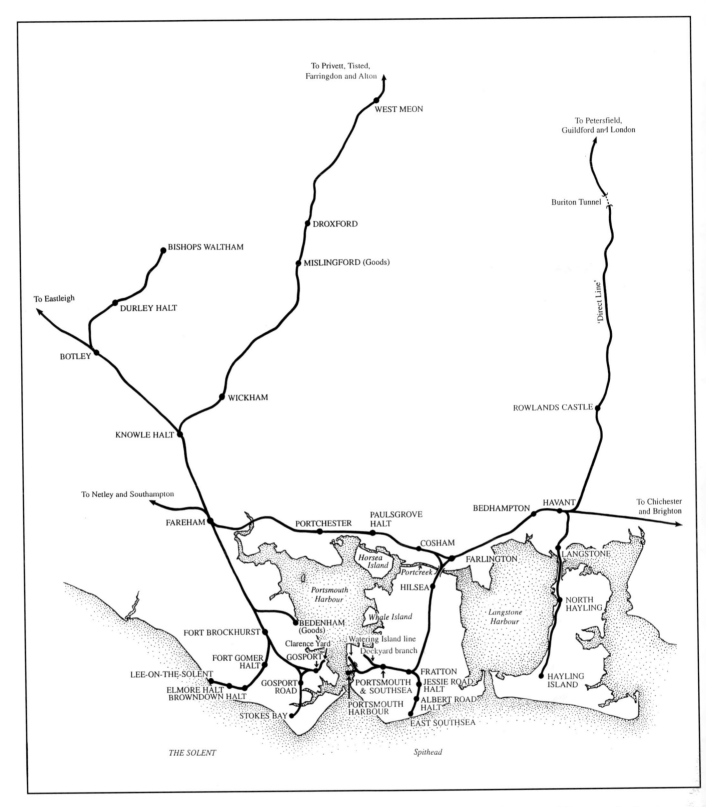

To Privett, Tisted,
Farringdon and Alton

WEST MEON

To Petersfield,
Guildford and London

Buriton Tunnel

DROXFORD

'Direct Line'

BISHOPS WALTHAM

MISLINGFORD (Goods)

To Eastleigh

DURLEY HALT

ROWLANDS CASTLE

BOTLEY

WICKHAM

KNOWLE HALT

To Netley and Southampton

BEDHAMPTON   HAVANT   To Chichester
and Brighton

FAREHAM   PORTCHESTER   PAULSGROVE
HALT   COSHAM   FARLINGTON   LANGSTONE

Horsea
Island   Portcreek

HILSEA   NORTH
HAYLING

Portsmouth
Harbour   Langstone
Harbour

Whale Island

FORT BROCKHURST   BEDENHAM
(Goods)   Watering Island line
Clarence Yard   Dockyard branch   HAYLING
ISLAND

FORT GOMER
HALT   GOSPORT   FRATTON

LEE-ON-THE-SOLENT   GOSPORT   PORTSMOUTH   JESSIE ROAD
ROAD   & SOUTHSEA   HALT

ELMORE HALT   PORTSMOUTH   ALBERT ROAD
BROWNDOWN HALT   HARBOUR   HALT

STOKES BAY   EAST SOUTHSEA

THE SOLENT   Spithead

Half title It is 14 December 1963 and the frost still lingers on the railway sleepers as Standard Class '4' 2-6-0 No 76028 comes off the High Level platform with the 12 noon passenger train from Portsmouth Harbour to Cardiff. Note the 'Nelson' electric unit in the siding on the left, and, on the extreme left, the imposing structure of the Guildhall - a typical Portsmouth scene! *Bruce Oliver*

Above A map of railway lines around Portsmouth, showing many of the locations featured in the book; the many other narrow gauge and miniature railways, tramways and sidings referred to in the book are not shown. Fratton-allocated steam locomotives worked the majority of the lines shown, some right up to the demise of steam in the area in July 1967, although throughout the 1960s the engines were provided by Eastleigh since Fratton ceased to have its own allocation in 1959.

RAILWAY HERITAGE

PORTSMOUTH

Including lines to East Southsea, Gosport, Fareham, the Meon Valley, Bishops Waltham, and Havant to Hayling Island

150 years of railways around Britain's principal naval port

Michael G. Harvey
Eddie Rooke
Bruce Oliver

Silver Link Publishing Ltd

First published in November 1997
Reprinted September 1999

British Library Cataloguing in Publication Data

A catalogue record for this book is available from the British Library

ISBN 1 85794 104 7

Silver Link Publishing Ltd
The Trundle
Ringstead Road
Great Addington
Kettering
Northants
NN14 4BW

Tel/Fax: 01536 330588
email: sales@slinkp-p.demon.co.uk

Printed and bound in Great Britain

Map on page 2 drawn by Christina Siviter

BIBLIOGRAPHY

Reference has been made to the following books:

Bennett, A. *Southern Holiday Lines in Hampshire & Isle of Wight* (Runpast Publishing, 1994)

Bird, J. H. *Southern Steam Surrender* (Kingfisher Railway Productions, 1987)

Bolger, P. *BR Steam Motive Power Depots (SR)* (Ian Allan, 1983)

Cooper, P. *LBSCR Stock Book* (Runpast Publishing, 1990)

Cooper, B. K., and Antell, R. *LSWR: A Tribute to the London & South Western Railway* (Ian Allan, 1988)

Course, E. *Portsmouth Railways* (Portsmouth City Council, 1969)

Faulkner, J. N. and Williams, R. A. *The LSWR in the Twentieth Century* (David & Charles, 1988)

Glenn, D. F. *Rail Routes in Hampshire & East Dorset* (Ian Allan, 1983)

One Hundred Years of Roads and Rails Around The Solent (Ensign Publications, 1991)

Griffiths, R. *Southern Sheds in Camera* (Oxford Publishing Co, 1989)

Hawkins, C. and Reeve, G. *An Historical Survey of Southern Sheds* (Oxford Publishing Co, 1979)

London & South Western Railway Engine Sheds (Western District) (Irwell Press, 1990)

Keat, P. *Rails to the Yards* (Gosport Railway Society, 1994)

Middlemass, T. *Stroudley and his 'Terriers'* (Pendragon, 1995)

Mitchell, V. and Smith, K. *Branch Lines to Alton* (Middleton Press, 1984)

Branch Line to Hayling (Including The Isle of Wight Train Ferry) (Middleton Press, 1984)

South Coast Railways: Portsmouth to Southampton (Middleton Press, 1986)

Fareham to Salisbury via Eastleigh (Middleton Press, 1989)

South Coast Railways: Chichester to Portsmouth (Middleton Press, 1984)

Branch Lines Around Gosport (Middleton Press, 1986)

Reed, M. J. E. *The Island 'Terriers'* (Kingfisher Railway Productions, 1989)

Robertson, K. *The Railways of Gosport* (Kingfisher Railway Productions, 1986)

Russell, J. H. *A Pictorial Record of Southern Locomotives* (BCA/Haynes Publishing Group, 1991)

Simmonds and Robertson, K. *The Bishops Waltham Branch* (Wild Swan Publications, 1988)

Stone, R. A. *The Meon Valley Railway* (Kingfisher Railway Productions, 1983)

Various editions of the following magazines have also been consulted: *Railway Magazine*; *Railway World*; *Steam Railway*; *Steam World*; *Trains Illustrated*; *British Railways Illustrated*; *Steam Days*; *Railways South East*; together with various Ian Allan ABCs and *Trident* naval newspapers.

CONTENTS

Introduction   6

1. The railway arrives in Portsmouth   7
2. Main lines in the days of steam   11
3. Fratton locomotive depot   26
4. Naval establishments   43
5. Goods yards and sidings   53

6. Lost lines   60
7. Miscellaneous railways   88
8. Successors to steam   94
9. Steam returns to the city   122
10. The future - and opportunities lost?   126

Index of locations   128

ACKNOWLEDGEMENTS

To compile a book containing so many personal memories it has been necessary to seek the co-operation of a vast number of people, and it is hoped that everyone who contributed even in a small way is listed below. However, a mere mention of their name is insufficient gratitude to the following persons without whom the book would never have reached its final state:

Denis Callender: Although arriving on the scene at almost the last moment his photographic contributions have been much valued.

Alf Coffin: When this old Portmuthian contacted us with details of his photographs taken circa 1930 the book was in its final stages of preparation, but the opportunity to use such old, rare photographs was much appreciated.

Eric Grace: For the excellent photographs he has provided for the chapter on Fratton locomotive depot and throughout the book.

Bruce Oliver: For the large number of photographs he has provided together with his excellent local knowledge, upon which we have drawn heavily, as evidenced by Chapter 8, which he compiled.

Doug Willis: For his introductions to many ex-railwaymen and his willingness to convalesce following an operation by spending many hours in Portsmouth City Museum in order to peruse old records.

Jeff Wyncoll: For his efforts to put us in touch with his railway colleagues, and general all-round co-operation.

And in alphabetical order:

Pat Anderson, Roy Baker, Pete Barnett, Graham Beech, Alan A. F. Bell, Len Betts, Bill Bishop, George Blakey, Roger Bray, R. Casserley, Gary Chase, A. D. Davies, Tom H. J. Dethridge, Stuart Egbeare, Bob Gorringe, Bob Haddock, Norman Hamshere, Leslie Hanson, Richard G. Hardy, John Harris, Steve Hayward, Tanya Kapoor, Charles Kemp, George Lee, R. Leovold, Brian Moss, David L. Norman, Dave Pallett, Lynn Rooke, Colin Saunders, John Scutt, Bob Smith, John Spence, Ray A. Stone, Denis Tillman, Jennifer Trodd, Dave Watson and Brian Witts.

Our thanks also go to:

Ron Brown (*The NEWS*, Portsmouth), Chichester Records Office, Fareham Museum, Havant Museum, Brian Patterson (The Dockyard Historical Trust), Portsmouth City Museum, The National Railway Museum (York), The Science Museum (London), and Winchester Records Office.

If we have omitted anyone, please accept our apologies.

INTRODUCTION

Following the publication of the second volume of his book *Diary of a Train-spotter*, covering the years 1960 to 1968, Michael Harvey found himself in the position of having a vast amount of unpublished material relating in the main to the Portsmouth area. His personal train-spotting memoirs amounted to in excess of 800 pages, and it had been necessary to reduce this down to approximately 250 pages for publication. With the co-operation of his friend Eddie Rooke, who had made a substantial contribution to the preparation of Michael's first two books, it was therefore decided to utilise some of the excess material in another book.

The original intention was to put together a volume depicting the various types of steam locomotives used in the Portsmouth area during the 1950s and '60s. However, having made contact with a large number of ex-railwaymen and local enthusiasts, and having listened to their reminiscences, it was decided to widen the scope of the proposed book to cover the railway scene in the Portsmouth area from its very concept in the mid-19th century right through to the imminent dawning of the new Millennium.

Since the end of standard gauge steam on British Railways in 1968, a vast number of books have been published on a wide range of aspects of railways countrywide. It is, however, clear that Portsmouth has to a large extent been ignored by the railway press. Although the Gosport, Hayling and Meon Valley lines have all been the subject of separate books in recent years, so far Portsmouth only seems to have attracted the attention of the Middleton Press in their 'South Coast Railways' series of excellent pictorial histories.

This book endeavours to cover the birth of railways in the area and takes the reader on a relaxed journey through a century and a half of local railway history, bringing the story right up to date with the inclusion of photographs depicting the return of working steam locomotives to the area in the 1990s, together with further photographs portraying today's scenes on the long lost railways of Hayling Island, Gosport, the Meon Valley and Bishops Waltham.

Every effort has been made to ensure that the vast majority of the photographs used in this book are original and have not been published before. For this reason the reader will note that the bulk of them relate to the second half of the period covered, since regrettably our intensive research has revealed that the few early photographs that are available have all been used on at least one occasion in other publications, and it has always been our intention to ensure that the book has a 'fresh' feel about it. Accordingly, we have resisted the temptation to plunder the files of the local newspapers for photographs.

Finally, it is acknowledged that Gosport did in fact acquire its railway almost six years before Portsmouth, but this book is being launched to celebrate the 150th anniversary of the arrival of the railway in the city of the title.

1.
THE RAILWAY ARRIVES IN PORTSMOUTH

Prior to the arrival in Portsmouth of the London, Brighton & South Coast Railway in 1847, there had been several abortive schemes to bring various forms of railways to the area.

The first recorded plans were drawn up in 1803 by R. A. Edlington, and were for a horse-drawn railway between London and Portsmouth, as was common around the time of the Napoleonic Wars in mining districts. In the same year a canal engineer named William Jessop undertook a survey for a route between Blackfriars (London) and Portsmouth, with estimated costs of £400,000. This line was planned to link with the Surrey Iron Railway, which had opened that year and operated between Wandsworth and Croydon using horse-drawn wagons. Neither of these plans came to fruition, and in any event the Surrey Iron Railway ceased operation in 1846.

In 1823 William James prepared a report highlighting the advantages of rail connections from London to the ports of Shoreham, Chatham and Portsmouth. Links were planned with, once again, the Surrey Iron Railway and the Croydon, Merstham & Godstone Railway (both horse railways). However, unlike the first two proposals, the operation of locomotives over some sections would have been probable, with stationary engines and cables being used to haul the trains up steeper gradients.

In 1838 there was yet another fruitless scheme for a direct line to the capital via Chichester, Arundel and Dorking, although this route was later adopted by the London, Brighton & South Coast Railway.

In 1844 the idea of an atmospheric railway between London and Portsmouth was mooted. This system relied upon a continuous trackside tube with pumping stations at regular intervals to create and maintain a vacuum; a cylinder attached to the train was drawn through the tube at speeds in excess of 40 mph. However, although the London & Croydon Railway started a service between Croydon and Forest Hill in 1846, the scheme was short-lived and was abandoned.

Meanwhile the London & South Western Railway (formerly the London & Southampton Railway) had completed its line to Southampton in 1840, while the London & Brighton Railway (which became the London, Brighton & South Coast Railway in 1846) reached Brighton in the following year. Prior to the completion of these lines, both companies, as well as other independent companies, had planned routes into Portsmouth. In 1836 the Portsmouth Junction Railway, which had links with the London & Southampton, deposited plans for a branch line from the latter's line at Eastleigh to Portsmouth via Fareham and Cosham - more or less in line with the present-day route - together with another line from Fareham to Gosport. However, Portsmouth Corporation objected to Parliament on the basis that a direct route to London was preferable to a route via Southampton that incurred extra mileage.

Opposition to these plans weakened over the next couple of years, and with the London & Southampton Railway being diplomatically renamed the London & South Western (there was intense rivalry between Portsmouth and Southampton even in those days), objections to the branch line from Southampton were dropped on the understanding that Portsmouth could still have a direct line to the capital. Accordingly, the LSWR's bill for lines to Portsmouth and Gosport received Royal Assent in June 1839. The line to Gosport opened on 29 November 1841, only to close four days later as a result of the collapse of a tunnel north of Fareham. It opened fully the following February.

Unfortunately this did not signal the imminent arrival of the railway in Portsmouth; for five years the inhabitants of Portsmouth had to cross Portsmouth Harbour to catch the train at Gosport - a somewhat ironic reversal of the position that has obtained since 1953 when Gosport's inhabitants lost their railway. A further disadvantage of the lack of a railway into Portsmouth was the loss of some foreign traffic into the port from such countries as France and India, which preferred the growing port of Southampton because of its rail links.

The development of Portsmouth was clearly being hampered by the delay in providing a railway, and it was not until 14 June 1847 that the LBSCR finally completed its line from Brighton into Portsmouth to become the very first railway company into Portsmouth. Meanwhile, the LSWR, which would probably have been content to route all of its traffic into Gosport rather than construct a line into Portsmouth, had its hand forced by other companies' plans for the city and in 1844 submitted to Parliament fresh plans to reach the town - first via Fareham and Cosham and secondly via Guildford, Godalming, Midhurst and Chichester. Around the same time plans were also deposited by other companies in the form of the Direct London & Portsmouth, the Brighton & Chichester Railway (Portsmouth Extension) and the London & Portsmouth. The local Corporation gave its support to the Direct London & Portsmouth, but, after much debate, the only bill to pass through the House of Lords was that for the eastern route from Brighton, for which Royal Assent was given on 8 August 1845.

Undeterred, the Direct London & Portsmouth (by then an amalgamation of the London & Croydon and the London & Brighton companies) and the LSWR tried once again with their bills, which resulted in Royal Assents being obtained on 26 June and 27 July 1846 respectively. The LSWR was to be allowed use of the proposed direct line and was authorised to build a link from its terminus at Guildford to a junction with the new line at Godalming. Prospects of a railway into Portsmouth were now looking much improved with three lines now authorised. However, whereas the other two more or less followed the line of today's route into the city, the LSWR's plans envisaged a line down the west side of Portsea Island, passing between Landport and the Dockyard before arriving at a terminus by Unicorn Gate, from where short branch lines would be built to the Dockyard and the junction of Union Road (later Commercial Road) and Edinburgh Road to serve Southsea. Unfortunately, financial backing was hard to obtain at that time and a major detrimental factor was the demand by the Military Authority for the sum of £12,000 to permit the breaching of the town's fortifications at Hilsea.

The LBSCR had built Hilsea Redoubt at Hilsea Lines when it had been allowed to breach the fortifications by the Board of Ordnance and had crossed Portcreek initially by a wooden viaduct built in 1846 and subsequently replaced in 1870 by a swing bridge. This enabled the LBSCR (who had reached Havant on 15 March 1847) to open its line into Portsmouth on Saturday 14 June 1847. However, this did not go too smoothly as evidenced by the following extract from a report in *The Hampshire Telegraph* of 19 June 1847:

'THE LONDON, BRIGHTON, AND SOUTH COAST RAILWAY - Although not formally announced by advertisement to take place, the Portsmouth Extension was opened for traffic on Monday last; engines having been brought from Brighton on the previous day to this terminus preparatory thereto. To show what we deem the undue haste with which this line was opened, we may mention that in coming down, owing to the road having been raised since the bridge at Fratton, under which the rail passes, was erected, the chimney of one of the engines struck the bridge; and before the trains started on Monday morning it was necessary to lower the road at this spot. This oversight argues great carelessness somewhere. The appearance of the engines employed on this line bears no comparison with that of the engines used on the line with which this company competes; they may be efficient, but judging from their shabby exterior, they are old. The trains have continued to run regularly, and have kept their time during the week.'

From the outset it was quite clear that the one line on Portsea Island was quite adequate to deal with the volume of traffic emanating from the LBSCR in the east and the LSWR in the west. Accordingly the two companies agreed to share the line, the LSWR abandoned its authorised western approach into the town, and in turn the LBSCR dropped its plans for a line from Cosham to Fareham. The 4½ miles between Cosham and Portsmouth were jointly managed by the LSWR and the LBSCR companies, with passenger traffic receipts being pooled then shared, after deductions for expenses, in proportions of five-eighths to the LSWR and three-eighths to the LBSCR.

A famous Portsmouth character

One of Britain's greatest engineering personalities, Isambard Kingdom Brunel, was born in Britain Street, Old Portsmouth, in 1806. He was the son of Marc Brunel, also an engineer of great repute. Today Britain Street no longer exists and no trace remains of his birthplace.

I. K. Brunel was given the title of Engineer to the Great Western Railway in 1833. In 1841 his original train shed terminus at Bristol (Temple Meads) station was completed, and still stands today, albeit not in use as a station. Also preserved in Bristol is his magnificent steamship *Great Britain*, the first iron ship to cross the Atlantic. Another Bristol landmark is Brunel's masterpiece in bridge design and construction, the Clifton Suspension Bridge, opened in 1864.

The LSWR line from Fareham to Cosham was opened to goods traffic on 1 September 1848 and the first passenger train into Portsmouth on this route ran one month later on 1 October. So at last Portsmouth had a viable rail service to London, albeit in a rather roundabout way, with a route mileage of just under 100 miles, whether you chose to travel via Eastleigh or Brighton - some 20 miles or so more than the direct route of today. Journey times amounted to 3 or 4 hours and, probably on account of the receipts-pooling arrangements by the two companies, there was no competition and no incentive to improve timings!

Consequently there was still a demand for the building of a direct line to London, for which the LBSCR still had authorisation. In 1852 the speculative Portsmouth Railway deposited plans for a line from Godalming (which had been linked with Guildford in 1849) to Havant via Haslemere and Petersfield, and these were authorised on 8 July 1853. This company had the support of the people of Portsmouth and the well-known contractor Thomas Brassey attracted sufficient capital, without enlisting assistance from the other railway companies, to build a single track (it was doubled by 1877) along a difficult curving route with many severe gradients that proved difficult for steam locomotives. Authority to build a separate line from Havant to Hilsea was never followed through.

Although the LSWR was initially reluctant to get involved for fear of antagonising the LBSCR (it was, in any event, quite content with its existing longer route to London, since fares were based on mileage!), it eventually became so concerned that other railway companies might lease or purchase the line that it decided to lease it itself to protect its own interests.

This decision caused problems from the outset. The people of Portsmouth had always backed the building of the line and were incensed when they learned that it was the intention to charge the same fare for this new 74-mile route as on the old circuitous 95-mile route. Accordingly they raised a petition against the bill that leased the line to the LSWR, and Parliament was sufficiently moved to insert certain protective clauses into the bill to protect the interests of the people of Portsmouth.

This is William James Martin, a ticket collector employed by the London, Brighton & South Coast Railway in 1902 - and what a smart uniform! He had the distinction of being the first person to go through Buriton Tunnel on the Portsmouth Direct Line, not by train or on foot but being pushed on his hands and knees! As he was of 'skinny' build, it was agreed that he be chosen to open up the 'first daylight' when the final section of earth was being removed from the tunnel!

His other achievements include helping to build the former viaduct on the Hayling Island branch and helping out with station duties at Havant as a volunteer during the General Strike of 1926.

Photograph by kind permission of Elsie Abbott (née Martin)

The following extract is taken from *The Hampshire Telegraph* of Saturday 26 June 1847:

TO RAILWAY TRAVELLERS AND OTHERS.

A DINNER is provided every day at HOGG'S RAILWAY TAVERN, one hundred yards from the Portsmouth Terminus of the South Coast Railway. The Chair is taken by the Host at 15 minutes before one o'clock punctually.

DINNER ONE SHILLING; Wines and Spirits of the finest quality.

The accommodation at this Tavern is really of a superior description, and embraces clean, scrupulously clean, Bed-rooms, a liberal provision for the table; it is in fact as nearly as possible like your own home.

If you doubt it come and dine with us and see our arrangements.

A Porter and Servants up at five o'clock, and Breakfasts provided before the departure of the first trains.

Omnibuses, Flys, and Vans always ready.

MODERATE, STRICTLY MODERATE, CHARGES!

The LSWR had incorrectly assumed that once the line opened for business it would be entitled to use the LBSCR line between Havant and Portcreek Junction without any difficulty. The LBSCR, however, did not agree, and the outcome was 'the Battle of Havant', followed by a prolonged court case.

On 28 December 1858 the LSWR decided to assert what it thought to be its rights by sending a goods train down the line powered by Beattie-designed 2-4-0 engines at each end. However, on arrival at Havant the train stopped on account of the blocking of the line by a Bury-designed 0-4-0 goods engine chained to the rails together with the removal of a section of railway track! Some reports of the ensuing events appear to have been exaggerated, and although it seems certain that LSWR navvies attempted to remove the obstructing locomotive, there was never any major violence between the two parties.

The argument was subsequently transferred to the courts; in the meantime the LSWR commenced its service on New Year's Day 1859, utilising a temporary halt at Denvilles (just north of Havant station) and transporting its passengers into Portsmouth by means of a four-horse-drawn omnibus.

By 24 January 1859 the courts had found in the LSWR's favour, permitting the first through trains on the Direct Line into Portsmouth. However, the LBSCR lodged an appeal and for the very first time embarked upon a period of competition with its rival company by cutting fares and timings together with other incentives. The court gave a reserved judgement on the LBSCR appeal in June 1859 and the LSWR was forced once again to use the temporary halt at Denvilles. However, with both companies 'feeling the pinch' on account of the loss in revenue through the fare-cutting competition, agreement was reached to re-instate the previous system of pooling receipts that existed in 1848. In addition, the LSWR had to pay the LBSCR £2,500 per annum to use the line from Havant to Portcreek, while the Brighton company agreed to pay £15,000 per annum towards the LSWR's rental costs on the Direct Line . . . a short-lived situation since the LSWR soon absorbed the line.

So in 1859 Portsmouth at long last had its direct connection to London, and a total of three lines running into the town. Excursion traffic seemed very popular and there are reports of 2,000 people arriving in a 42-coach train hauled by three steam locomotives down the Direct Line!

Smarting a little at the use by the LSWR of the Direct Line, the LBSCR was soon building its own shorter route to London, and in 1867 opened an 87-mile route to London Bridge via Pulborough and Dorking (a reduction of 8 miles).

An advertisement carried in the Portsmouth *Evening News* on 17 July 1867:

REFRESHMENT ROOM - RAILWAY STATION
PORTSMOUTH

SOUPS - HOT JOINTS - VEGETABLES -
CHEESE AND ATTENTIONS
2 SHILLINGS
DAILY   ONE-THREE

SOUPS - ENTREES - CHOPS - STEAKS - AT
ANY TIME.

SECOND CLASS: PLATE OF COLD MEAT
AND BREAD - 7d.

SANDWICH AND A GLASS OF ALLSOPPS
BURTON ALE - 3d.

WINES AND SPIRITS OF BEST QUALITY

JOHN S. HOUGHTON PROP:
AGENT FOR ALLSOPPS AND SONS PALE
AND BURTON ALE.

In 1876 the Military Authorities at last relented and allowed the fortifications to be breached to allow the construction of the line from the Town station to Portsmouth Harbour, with the resultant increase in holiday traffic to the Isle of Wight.

In the years that followed there was little railway expansion outside the town to affect Portsmouth other than the Meon Valley Line of 1903 (of which more detail is given in Chapter 6)

In 1885 a circular route was proposed from the Southsea Branch at Fratton eastwards to cross Langstone Harbour and link up with the Hayling line - a distance of 3½ miles. The cost would have been £84,000, largely accounted for by the expense of approach roads and the bridge between the two islands. Although Parliament approved the bill in September 1886, matters did not proceed and one can only imagine what the long-term effect would have been on Hayling Island had the plans come to fruition - today's modest population and large open areas would, no doubt, have changed radically.

The LSWR and LBSCR were amalgamated in 1923 to form part of the Southern Railway, and it was this company that carried through plans to electrify, by the addition of a third rail, many of the routes from 1937 onwards. This vastly changed the railway scene around Portsmouth, and is dealt with in more detail in Chapter 8.

2.
MAIN LINES IN THE DAYS OF STEAM

The routes out of Portsmouth are initially not too demanding on motive power. With the city being virtually flat, the only real incline is the 1 in 61 at Portsmouth & Southsea High Level station, giving access to the line to the Harbour station, this section of line being built throughout on an elevated embankment.

Today Portsmouth (originally known as Portsea Island) has four railway stations - Portsmouth Harbour, Portsmouth & Southsea, Fratton, and Hilsea - the three stations on the former East Southsea branch line having closed early in the century. Although not generally recognised by the public, a station platform did exist on the approach to Unicorn Gate on the Dockyard branch. Although it is an island, Portsmouth can claim two terminus stations - Portsmouth & Southsea Low Level and Portsmouth Harbour - both within a mile of each other.

Moving off Portsea Island the line splits at Cosham triangle, with Cosham to the west and Havant to the east. The route through Cosham via Portchester to Fareham runs along the base of Portsdown Hill and gradients are slight before the line enters Fareham via the large viaduct that is featured in this chapter. For a few years before the Second World War there was a halt at Paulsgrove to serve the racecourse there, and in recent years there have been discussions between Hampshire County Council and Railtrack about re-instating a facility for the Paulsgrove housing estate in this area.

Heading east from Cosham triangle there was once a station at Farlington; opened in 1891, when it finally closed in 1937 it was merely of 'halt' status and, once again, was originally built to serve the racecourse adjacent to the station. Bedhampton remains a busy station, while Havant station, substantially rebuilt before the Second World War and now no longer the junction station for the Hayling Island branch, serves a very wide catchment area including the massive Leigh Park estate; once again the County Council has considered the possibility of a new station at West Leigh.

Travelling from Havant via Rowlands Castle to Petersfield, the route is much more demanding, with the need to penetrate the South Downs; perhaps the most notable feature is Buriton Tunnel.

Hopefully the photographs and captions in this chapter, augmented by those in Chapter 8 depicting more modern traction over the same routes, will provide the reader with an interesting selection of nostalgic recollections.

Maunsell-designed Class 'U1' 2-6-0 No A893 is pictured on 6 August 1931 backing on to its train at Portsmouth Harbour station. This engine was built at Eastleigh Works in that year and several of the class were allocated to Fratton depot for the Waterloo fast and semi-fast services, with which, it is reported, they had difficulty in coping. *Leslie Hanson*

Adams-designed Class 'X2' 4-4-0 locomotive No 590 arrives at Portsmouth Harbour station with the 9.07 am service from Netley on 26 October 1935. Built in 1891, the locomotive was withdrawn in 1937. *H. C. Casserley*

Just arrived on the 11.50 am passenger train from Waterloo on 22 May 1937 is probably Maunsell's finest design of locomotive in the form of 'Schools' Class 4-4-0 No 933 *King's Canterbury*. Ten of this class were allocated to Fratton depot immediately prior to third rail electrification of the line to Waterloo (July 1937), and during the relatively short time that they worked this route they performed in an excellent fashion, reducing previous scheduled timings by 8 minutes.

On 24 February 1957 the Locomotive Club of Great Britain ran a tour entitled 'Southern Counties Limited', which, after a trip over the Hayling Island branch, staged a magnificent finale by returning to the pre-war steam age on the Portsmouth line with a 90-minute non-stop run from Portsmouth Harbour station to Waterloo behind No 30929 *Malvern* with a six-coach load of 197 tons. The train ran just ahead of schedule the whole way, reaching Waterloo 1 minute early. Three of the class of 40 locomotives survive in preservation. *H. C. Casserley*

A rarity in Portsmouth! LNER Class 'B1' 4-6-0 No 61200 of Kings Cross depot found its way to Portsmouth Harbour station on 17 July 1961 with an excursion from New Southgate, London. It is seen awaiting its return trip. Eastern Region locomotives were exceptionally rare visitors to Portsmouth, although classmate No 61119, allocated to Stratford, London, was recorded on 6 May 1959. *Bruce Oliver*

On the final day of 1966 a pair of Standard Class '5' 4-6-0s, Nos 73065 and 73043, reverse down from Portsmouth & Southsea High Level towards Fratton depot for coal and water, having hauled their special train into Portsmouth Harbour station. *Bruce Oliver*

Standard Class '5' 4-6-0 locomotive No 73043 raises steam at Portsmouth & Southsea Low Level on 31 July 1963 prior to its departure with the 10.34 am passenger train to Bristol (Temple Meads). *Bruce Oliver*

An unidentified Standard Class '4' 2-6-0 locomotive is pictured at Canal Walk in April 1963 with the Portsmouth portion of the Brighton/Portsmouth to Plymouth train. This stretch of line was formerly part of the Portsmouth & Arundel Canal. *Bruce Oliver*

Left On Trafalgar Day, 21 October 1937, splendidly turned out Maunsell Class 'LN' 4-6-0 locomotive No 850 *Lord Nelson* certainly attracts some admirers at Portsmouth & Southsea Low Level station. In fact this was an exhibition train that became virtually an annual feature in the 1930s at this station to mark Trafalgar Day. These static displays proved to be a tremendous attraction to the general public, and were either sponsored by a firm such as Fry's Chocolate or consisted of a selection of the Southern's up-to-date designs of passenger stock on view for the public to browse around. *Alf Coffin*

Below left Drummond-designed Class 'L12' 4-4-0 No 429 is seen at the engine turntable and servicing area at Portsmouth & Southsea, in a view taken from 'Jacob's Ladder'. This site remained intact until the end of BR steam in Portsmouth in July 1967. *Norman Hamshere collection*

Top right Class 'U' 2-6-0 No 31803 heads the 6.02 pm parcels train from Portsmouth & Southsea Low Level (possibly to a Midlands destination) as it approaches Somers Road Bridge on 31 July 1963. In the final years of steam this class of locomotive, together with BR Standards, carried out the bulk of passenger workings in the Portsmouth area. *Bruce Oliver*

Right Class 'S15' 4-6-0 No 30840 reverses its empty stock past Fratton West signal box on its way to Fratton carriage sidings on 31 July 1963. *Bruce Oliver*

Right Snow in Portsmouth has always been rare. This Boxing Day 1962 picture shows Class 'U' 2-6-0 locomotive No 31624 backing its carriages past Fratton West signal box to Portsmouth & Southsea (Low Level) station to form the 12.15 pm passenger train to Plymouth, which it will take as far as Fareham. *Bruce Oliver*

With a Gresley coach directly behind the tender, 'ex-works' Class 'K' 2-6-0 No 32353 eases into Fratton station having just passed under Fratton Road bridge. Two of these handsome Billinton-designed locomotives were allocated to Fratton depot during its final years - primarily for freight duties - and they were highly regarded by Fratton drivers. *Bruce Oliver*

Class 'N15' ('King Arthur') 4-6-0 No 30773 *Sir Lavaine* performs empty stock duties at Fratton station in April 1961. *Bruce Oliver*

GWR 'Hall' Class 4-6-0 No 5932 *Haydon Hall* enters Fratton station on 31 August 1963 with the 3.48 pm Portsmouth Harbour to Wolverhampton through train. This class of locomotive was the most common of ex-GW visitors to Portsmouth, although excursion traffic frequently provided 'Grange' and '4300' Classes and even the occasional 'Manor' in the 1950s and '60s. *Bruce Oliver*

On 12 August 1931 a regular visitor, in the form of 4-4-0 No 3323 *Etona*, awaits departure from platform 1 at Fratton station with the afternoon return working to Reading General. Prior to the arrival of the 'Hall' Class 4-6-0s it was possible both to turn and service the 'Bulldogs' at Portsmouth & Southsea using the turntable and other facilities there. *Leslie Hanson*

On 5 August 1931 Adams Class 'X6' 4-4-0 No E661 has just passed Kingston Recreation Ground with a passenger train and is approaching Fratton station. Introduced in 1895, this particular engine was withdrawn in 1936. *Leslie Hanson*

With only one week of BR steam-operated trains in Portsmouth remaining, this 3 July 1967 picture portrays a typical scene at Fratton East signal box with a Standard Class locomotive employed on van duties. Another Standard - Class '4' 2-6-0 No 76007 - is in the sidings, while on the extreme left we catch a glimpse of a Class 33 diesel in the goods yard, and some electric units can be seen in sidings to the right of the goods van. *Bruce Oliver*

Above Having just passed under St Mary's Road bridge, Maunsell Class 'N' 2-6-0 No 31410 drifts past Kingston Recreation Ground with a goods train in the early 1960s. The track to the right of the picture was connected directly to Fratton goods yard. *Eric Grace*

Left Standard Class '5' 4-6-0 No 73111 is pictured on 31 July 1963 having just passed Burrfields Sports Ground, south of Hilsea Gas Works, with a passenger train bound for Portsmouth. *Bruce Oliver*

Green Lanes Crossing signal box was situated at Hilsea Gas Works and controlled the level crossing gates that gave access to the gas works across the main lines. The crossing closed in 1976 and both signal box and gates have since been removed. *Graham Beech*

On 21 April 1951, with Portsdown Hill forming the background, Drummond-designed Class 'D15' 4-4-0 passenger locomotive No 30471 rounds the curve of Cosham triangle heading for Portsmouth with a train from Cardiff. Prior to the arrival of new Class 'U1' 2-6-0s in 1931, Fratton depot had the whole class of ten 'D15' engines allocated there, but because of the depot's short turntable it was necessary for them to operate with 3,500-gallon tenders instead of their usual 4,500-gallon examples. Built in 1912 and 1913, the 'D15s' lasted until the mid-1950s, when they were all withdrawn. They had a reputation for being fast, easy steaming locomotives. *Denis Callender*

After the Second World War, to cover a shortage of motive power, the Southern Region took 50 Class 'WD' (War Department) 2-8-0 freight locomotives on loan, and these were distributed around a variety of depots such as Brighton, Feltham, Redhill and Bricklayers Arms. Here we see Brighton-allocated engine No 77270 on freight duties leaving the goods yard at Cosham station. *Denis Callender*

Above Having just left Cosham station in the early 1950s is Marsh-designed 'Atlantic' Class 'H2' 4-4-2 No 32421 *South Foreland.* This class of locomotive performed regularly on cross-country passenger workings to and from Brighton, using the north side of the Cosham triangle to bypass Portsmouth. *Denis Callender*

Below Heading west out of Cosham station in the early 1950s is one of Wainwright's Class 'L' 4-4-0 locomotives, No 31778. At about this date a small batch of these locomotives was temporarily allocated to Eastleigh depot to cover a shortage of motive power. The bridge above the first carriage was originally used by the Horndean Light Railway and was demolished many years ago. *Denis Callender*

On 13 July 1964 rather grimy looking Maunsell Class 'S15' 4-6-0 No 30843 is on an Eastleigh to Chichester freight working at Cow Lane, just west of Cosham station. The chalk pits of Portsdown Hill (412 feet) can be clearly seen behind the train together with the Admiralty Research Establishment on the brow of the hill. *Bruce Oliver*

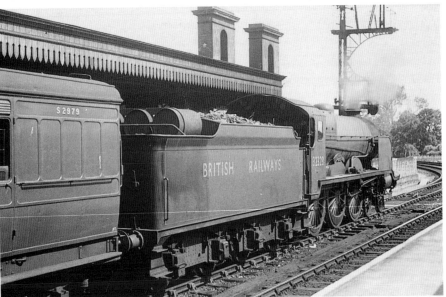

Above Crossing Fareham Viaduct with a Brighton to Plymouth train in the late 1940s is one of Bulleid's 'Battle of Britain' 4-6-2 locomotives, No 21C 149 (later renumbered to 34049) *Anti-Aircraft Command*. This particular engine enjoyed only a short life; built at Brighton Works in 1946, it was withdrawn from service in 1963. *Denis Callender*

Left Waiting to leave Fareham on 11 June 1949 with a Reading to Portsmouth train is Class 'N15X' 4-6-0 No 32328 *Hackworth*. This class of seven engines was also known as the 'Remembrance' Class, having been rebuilt from redundant 4-6-4 tanks between 1934 and 1936; they survived about 20 years in their rebuilt state. *Denis Callender*

In June 1951 this Plymouth to Brighton cross-country working is headed by Bulleid 'West Country' 4-6-2 No 34040 *Crewkerne*, seen here departing from Fareham station. *Crewkerne* was rebuilt in 1960 before being withdrawn in 1967. *Denis Callender*

Above A rare picture of a 'double-header' in the area on 2 July 1949. A pair of veteran Drummond-designed 4-4-0s, Class 'S11' No 395 and 'D15' No 30472, await departure from Fareham station. *Denis Callender*

Below On 6 April 1966 Standard Class '5' 4-6-0 No 73119 arrives at Fareham station with the through train from Cardiff to Brighton. *Bruce Oliver*

On 17 September 1966 the world-famous Gresley 'Pacific', No 4472 *Flying Scotsman*, is pictured near Bedhampton with an enthusiasts' special train from London to Eastleigh via Brighton and Havant. *Eric Grace*

Right One of Maunsell's 'U1' 2-6-0s, No 1899, pulls away from the old station at Havant with a Portsmouth Harbour to London (Waterloo) train *circa* 1932. *Alf Coffin*

Below This unidentified class 'T9' 4-4-0 is employed on a passenger working and is seen entering Havant old station *circa* 1932. The junction signals indicate the London line (left) and the Brighton line (right). The signal box controlled the main lines and the Hayling Island branch, from which the line on the right leads into the station bay platform. The short length of track with the buffer stops in front of the signal box was used to stable the Class 'A1X' tank engine employed on the Hayling Island branch in between duties. *Alf Coffin*

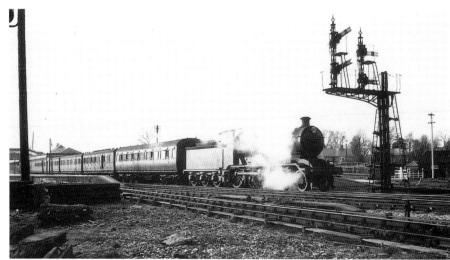

There's plenty of steam in this action picture of Class 'B4X' 4-4-0 No 2070 as it restarts a Brighton line train away from the up platform at the old Havant station, also *circa* 1932. This engine survived until 1951. *Alf Coffin*

3.
FRATTON
LOCOMOTIVE DEPOT

In 1889 plans were drawn up by the LSWR and LBSCR to erect a new, much larger locomotive depot near Fratton station to replace the smaller four-road depot at Portsmouth Town station, which was by then proving inadequate for the increasing traffic demands. Early plans reveal that the LBSCR had the use of this depot during the latter part of the 1850s and that this was erected on the northern side of the line and east of 'Jacob's Ladder', a footbridge that joined Greetham Street to Railway View.

Taking into account the rivalry between the two companies, it seems probable that the LSWR had the use of a site on the opposite side of the track, a little closer to the station. This area contained a turntable with five sidings leading off from it, which were no doubt used to accommodate locomotives between their duties. A water tank was situated here, unusual in that the tank engines that resided at this location would travel beneath it to take on water - in the 1930s it was common to note an Adams Class 'T1' 0-4-4 tank on duty here.

The new depot at Fratton was completed in 1891 and, although jointly owned by the two companies, from the outset and until the Grouping in 1923 they used separate offices, coal stages and strictly allocated roads within the

roundhouse. It was in fact one of only two depots shared by separate companies, the other being Aberdeen (Ferryhill), which was shared by the Caledonian and North British companies. The adoption of the round-house principle was also most unusual for the companies concerned and, although commonplace on the Western Region and elsewhere, by the time British Railways came into being in 1948 the only two similar structures on the Southern Region were the semi-roundhouses at Guildford and Horsham.

Within the roundhouse at Fratton were 24 stabling points (this was later reduced to 23), which were accessed via a 50-foot turntable, the same size as the one at the Town station. This created problems as locomotives became progressively larger, and it was later necessary to install a line parallel to Goldsmith Avenue to create a triangle, thereby enabling larger locomotives to reverse back to Fratton from the Town station and turn by running past the rear of the depot, along the eastern side and out through the depot yard on to the main line.

Access to the depot for railway workers was either from Goldsmith Avenue or over a footbridge, situated behind Walmer Road, which crossed the main lines at the front of the depot, adjacent to Fratton East signal box. Facilities at the depot were limited, although there was a hoist at the rear of the depot that enabled locomotives to be lifted to remove their wheels, etc.

The importance of Fratton locomotive depot declined after third rail electrification in 1937, prior to which time it had over 70 steam locomotives in its allocation. The accompanying table gives an indication of the types of motive power allocated there during its last ten years of

On 17 May 1920 the well-known and highly respected photographer H. C. Casserley visited Portsmouth for the first time and photographed Adams Class '0415' 4-4-2T No 481 in the roundhouse. These locomotives were introduced in 1883 and were used on passenger duties. This particular engine was withdrawn in 1924, but another example of this class survives today, preserved on the Bluebell Railway in Sussex. *H. C. Casserley*

Allocations of steam locomotives at Fratton depot, 1948 to 1958

Class	Type	31.7.48	31.8.50	23.7.53	20.4.56	13.10.58
'T1'	0-4-4		30020			
'M7'	0-4-4	30027/45/54, 30480	30045/50/4, 30480	30023/51/4	30022/39, 30357	30039, 30356/7
'T9'	4-4-0	30113/4/5/8, 30280/7, 30303/5, 30314/38, 30731	30113/4/5/8/20, 30280/5, 30303/5/10/4, 30726/31/3	30726/30/2	30726/9/30/2	30732
'O2'	0-4-4			30207	30207	
'L11'	4-4-0	30164/70/2, 30413/4/41	30170/2, 30441			
'S11'	4-4-0	30400/1/2/4	30395/6/7, 30400/2			
'L12'	4-4-0	30417/25	30417/9/26/7			
'U'	2-6-0	31625, 31797	31805/9	31807/8/9	31637/8, 31805/7/8/9	31637/8, 31804/5/7, 31808/9
'N'	2-6-0	31831	31870			
'E1'	0-6-0	32153, 32690/1/4	32129, 32691/4	32138/9/51, 32694	32138/9, 32694	32139, 32694
'E4'	0-6-2	32490/2, 32505/59	32487	32479/95, 32509	32479/95, 32509	32479/95, 32509
'E5'	0-6-2			32568		
'C3'	0-6-0		32300/1/3/6			
'K'	2-6-0		32338/40	32349	32337/49	32337/49
'C2X'	0-6-0	32537/48/54		32548/9/50	32548/9/50	32458/9/50
'A1X'	0-6-0	32644/55/9, 32661/2	32646/55/61/2, 32677	32655/61/2, 32677	32650/61, 32677	32640/6/50, 32661/77/8
'D1'*	0-4-2		701S			
Totals		46 (includes 14 oil-burners)	50 (includes 12 oil-burners)	26	28	27

*Service loco

existence, prior to official closure on 2 November 1959, when its allocation of locomotives was transferred to such diverse depots as Eastleigh, Southampton Docks, Guildford, Brighton, Three Bridges and Norwood Junction.

Servicing of visiting locomotives continued from the end of 1959 right up to the very last day of steam on the Southern Region, Sunday 9 July 1967; indeed, on that day Standard Class '5' 4-6-0 No 73029 was serviced before leaving on a ten-coach empty stock working to Clapham Junction, and later that afternoon Class 'USA' 0-6-0 tank No 30072 steamed in from Guildford en route to Eastleigh for disposal.

Fratton locomotive depot (with the exception of the offices) was finally demolished in March 1969, leaving the servicing of all motive power to the adjacent electric multiple unit depot, which had been built over three decades earlier.

Saddle-tanks were very rare in the South of England and pictured here in Fratton depot yard on 4 June 1921 is Beyer Peacock Class '0330' 0-6-0ST No 335. These shunting engines were nicknamed 'Saddlebacks' and this particular example was built in 1876 and withdrawn in 1932, when it was sold to the East Kent Railway. *H. C. Casserley*

Locomotive portraits taken in 1932 by Alf Coffin

At the age of 18, and the proud owner of a Brownie box camera, Alf Coffin used to make regular visits to the rear of Fratton locomotive depot to photograph the steam engines that were easily viewed from Goldsmith Avenue. He did not take any photographs inside of the roundhouse, as his type of camera was unsuitable.

Above Billinton-designed Class 'B2X' 4-4-0 No 206 in its penultimate year of service. Prior to rebuilding from Class 'B2' between 1907 and 1916, the whole of this class of 25 engines was used on the Portsmouth to London route. This particular engine was built in 1897 and withdrawn in 1933; in 1903 and 1904 it was used unsuccessfully in oil-firing trials.

Right This Stroudley-designed Class 'D1' 0-4-2T, No 2626, was one of a class of 125 tanks built between 1873 and 1887. At first used mainly on London suburban traffic, many of the class were subsequently fitted for 'push-pull' working; locally the class was used on services such as the 'Chichester Motor'. Note the goods depot under construction on the extreme left.

An early picture of the famous *Stepney* (No 2655), immortalised in the 'Thomas the Tank Engine' books. In front of it is another Class 'A1X' 0-6-0 tank, No 2635, and behind the engines can clearly be seen the curve of part of the track forming the triangle used for turning locomotives.

No 1 on both the LSWR and the Southern Railway! Built in 1894 at Nine Elms Works, this Class 'T1' 0-4-4T locomotive was withdrawn in 1949. Although tanks of this class were frequently used on light passenger turns, for many years a 'T1' was resident at Portsmouth & Southsea station as station pilot, and was also used for shunting empty stock.

Two of the Marsh-designed Class 'H1' 'Atlantic' 4-4-2s, Nos 2038 *Portland Bill* and 2041 *Peveril Point*, stand at the rear of the roundhouse. This small class of five locomotives built in 1905 and 1906 was used mainly on express passenger services. No 2041 was withdrawn in 1944, while No 2038 lasted until 1951.

Drummond-designed Class 'K10' 4-4-0 No 138 was one of a class of 40 engines built at Nine Elms Works between 1901 and 1902, used on mixed traffic duties and nicknamed 'Small Hoppers'. This particular engine did not survive until nationalisation of the railways, being withdrawn in 1947.

LBSCR No 54 *Empress*: this Brighton-built Class 'B4' 4-4-0 had a very special duty on 2 February 1901 when, virtually brand new, it had the distinction of hauling Queen Victoria's funeral train from Fareham to London. It is pictured here as No 2054, and was withdrawn in 1951.

Sixty Class 'O2' 0-4-4T locomotives were built at Nine Elms Works between 1889 and 1895. Their main claim to fame is the fact that 23 of them were used on the Isle of Wight right up until the end of steam. In the final years of steam at Portsmouth, fellow class member No 30207 was employed for many years as a regular on the Dockyard Goods. No 185, pictured here, was withdrawn in 1940.

Class 'J2' No 2326 was a Marsh-designed 4-6-2 tank locomotive. Built in 1912 and originally named *Bessborough*, the engine had a relatively short life, being withdrawn in 1951.

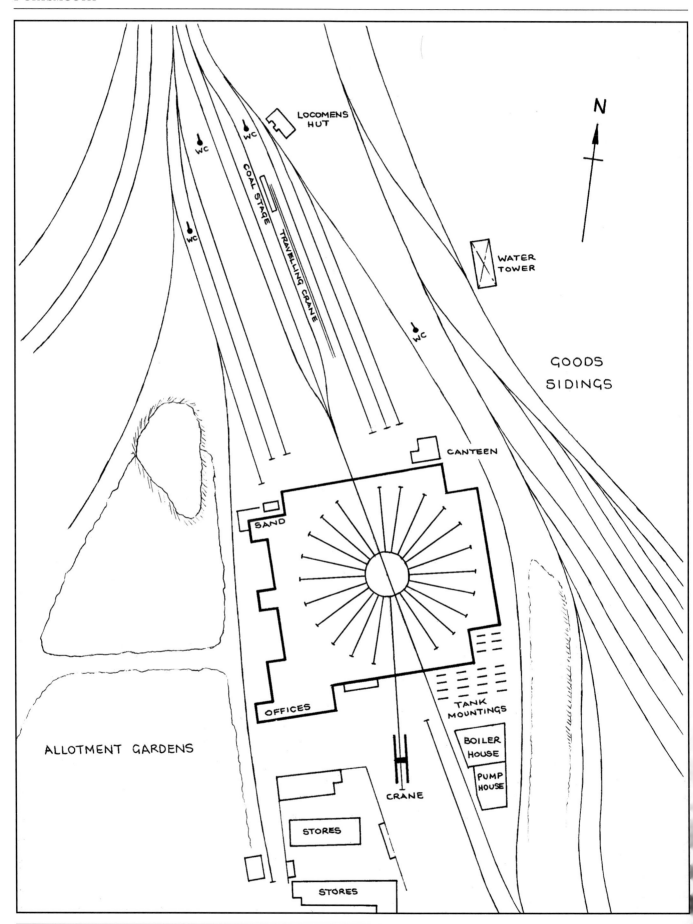

N

LOCOMENS HUT

WC

WC

WC

COAL STAGE

TRAVELING CRANE

WC

WATER TOWER

GOODS SIDINGS

CANTEEN

SAND

OFFICES

TANK MOUNTINGS

BOILER HOUSE

PUMP HOUSE

CRANE

ALLOTMENT GARDENS

STORES

STORES

Oil-burning locomotives

Just after the end of the Second World War the Government, concerned over the availability of coal supplies, enlisted the help of the railway companies in converting a proportion of steam locomotives to oil-burning. Both the LSWR and the Southern Railway had previous experience of this in 1921 and 1926 respectively, but this time the scheme was much more extensive. The Southern had plans to convert over 100 locomotives, but in fact only 31 were converted, and by the time the scheme was aborted in 1948 Fratton depot had became the sole fully operational fuelling depot on the Southern

Left A mid-1950s plan of Fratton locomotive depot. *Graham Beech*

Right As part of the scheme to convert a proportion of steam locomotives to oil-burning, a pump house was erected at the rear of Fratton locomotive depot. This can be seen to the left of this 1960 picture, with the roundhouse situated behind and to the right. *Michael G. Harvey*

(the Eastleigh and Exmouth Junction schemes were incomplete when the project was aborted).

Towards the end of 1948 Fratton's allocation of oil-burning 'T9' Class (Nos 113, 114, 115, 118, 280, 303, 305, 314 and 731) and 'L11' Class (Nos 170 and 172) were put 'in store', never to steam again - they were all withdrawn in 1951 and 1952 without being converted back to conventional coal-burning. Fratton's 'U' Class engines (Nos 1625 and 1797) and its solitary 'N' Class (No 1831) fared better, being restored to their original state and returned to service.

The following account details a Fratton railwayman's first-hand experience with the oil-burning scheme.

Memories of oil-burning locomotives

by George Blakey

As a cleaner and then a fireman based at Fratton engine shed, I still have vivid memories of some of the British Railways steam locomotives that were converted to oil-burning in an attempt to save coal at the end of the Second World War - and at the same time to help extend the working lives of those engines converted.

Oil-burners were first introduced in 1946 on the Southern Railway, and the first arrival at Fratton shed virtually appeared overnight, surprising everyone, although it was known that some engines were to be converted. The engine was 'King Arthur' Class No 740 *Merlin*. *Merlin* was used as a training engine but was limited in its use owing to not being allowed over the Netley line, which was involved in many of Fratton's duties. It was also too large for our 50-foot turntable. We then had a 'West Country' Class 4-6-2, No 34036 *Westward Ho!*, converted to oil-burning, and this was able to use the Netley road. Wash-outs were done at Fratton, achieved by splitting the engine from its tender - much to the disgust of the fitters, I suspect - although it may not have been such a messy job as a coal-burning engine.

Soon we had one of Drummond's 'T9' 4-4-0s, and

training continued for the shed fitters and firemen. The builders then arrived and began constructing a pump house and installing oil storage tanks; the pump house remained intact right up to the end of steam in the mid-1960s. Two redundant locomotive boilers were used to supply steam to a ring main that ran around the eastern half of the shed. At each end of 12 pits was a steam heating pipe coupling, and this enabled steam to be supplied to the oil-burning manifold on the footplate. The manifold had controls for the blower, steam atomiser, generator and tank heating - the oil fuel had to be kept at about 120 to 140 degrees F.

Oil-fired locomotives required far more concentration by the fireman than the coal-burning locomotives, since one had to continually monitor the smoke, adjusting the oil supply and steam to the atomiser and blower. The blower had always been on the driver's side of the engine and under his control; it was not unknown, as a result of this new system, for the fireman to forget that most vital of ingredients - the boiler water - and although I do not know of anyone actually coming to grief, I believe that there were some near-misses.

One mishap that did occur was inside the depot roundhouse when a fire-lighter, who is still alive today, and therefore shall be nameless, lit up the 12 oil-burning engines. By the time he got to the final engine the first one would normally be coming into steam, so he could sit down for a while before going back to the first engine and checking it over. On this occasion, being a warm night, he dropped off to sleep, and the first engine must have been a bit warmer than usual when it was put away, so steam rose a little faster than normal. This meant that the atomiser steam pressure had risen to a point where it in fact blew the flame out - but, of course, it still continued to atomise the oil, producing a yellow pungent gas and a stream of hot oil into the pit under the engine.

A fireman saw what was happening and shouted to the sleeping fire-lighter - somewhat startled, the man went over to the engine and proceeded to relight the flame without ensuring that all the gas had been purged out of the firebox. The result was a huge explosion of the gas and the ignition of a lot of hot oil in the pit, which did an enormous amount of damage to the motion and bearings before the shed staff were able to move the engine! Coincidentally, the engine was a 'T9' that was standing in the same road that 'T9' No 118 had been in some six years previous, when she was hit by a German bomb!

One thing that was noticeable was that, with the exception of the 'West Country' Class, oil-burning engines were very cold in the winter on the footplate; of course, unlike coal-burners their fire-doors were always *closed*. Some classes, such as the 'L11' 4-4-0s, were given

a new lease of life; as coal burners they were always a bit asthmatic, but when the experiment ceased most of them were scrapped.

The oil-burners were fitted with electric lighting for headcodes and footplate illumination - when reversion back to coal-firing came, the lighting was removed, which was a pity. I believe that the generators were fitted to the 'West Country' and 'Battle of Britain' engines that were still being built.

The experiment came to an end, I suspect, without too many tears. While I was in the Middle East working on army railways with oil-burning engines, the reasons given were that oil was as costly as coal, supplies could not be assured, there was a desperate shortage of foreign currency and that engines with copper fireboxes suffered more wear and tear than coal-fired engines.

Of course, the surges of heat required could not have been beneficial, but in my experiences on army locomotives (LMS Class '8F' 2-8-0s) there was no significant increase in stay leakage - and there were many other countries operating oil-fired locomotives successfully. Even today we have the Ffestiniog Railway in Wales operating with numerous oil-fired locomotives.

Finally, I wonder what would have been the outcome had North Sea oil been discovered sooner?

Stroudley Class 'D1' 0-4-2T No 700S (Service locomotive), the former Southern Railway No 2244, is sandwiched between oil tanker SM 1680 (Shell Mex) and the tender of a steam locomotive converted to oil-burning in Fratton depot yard, pictured in the mid-1940s. No 700S was used to pump oil out of the tanker and into the tenders of the oil-burning engines (note the pipes fitted to its coal bunker and along its running plate) - this procedure continued until the pump house was built at Fratton depot in 1947. No 700S was in fact allocated to Eastleigh, and sister engine No 701S (also a Class 'D1' tank, the former BR No 2284) was allocated to Fratton depot. Other engines from this class were additionally equipped with fire-fighting apparatus, and one was kept on constant standby at Fratton depot during the Second World War to help combat any threat of fire caused by bomb damage. *Lens of Sutton*

A Drummond-designed locomotive, Class 'L11' 4-4-0 No 170, also converted to oil-burning, is seen east of Cosham station, running 'light engine' to Fratton depot *circa* 1948. These engines were known as 'Hoppers', and a total of 40 were built between 1903 and 1907. Initially they were used on semi-fast and relief express workings, but in their later years were relegated to shorter-haul passenger and goods duties. *Denis Callender*

Only two of Maunsell's Class 'U' 2-6-0 locomotives were converted to oil-burning, and after the experiment was curtailed they were restored to conventional coal-burning. Although No 31625 was withdrawn from traffic in 1964, it was rescued from Barry scrapyard by the Mid-Hants Railway (the 'Watercress Line') and is pictured here at Ropley station in the autumn of 1996 having just been restored to running order for the first time for over three decades. *Eddie Rooke*

Right When staff at Fratton depot were sent to work at other depots this official form had to be completed. *Brian Moss collection*

Steam engines named after localities in the Portsmouth area

At the time of Grouping (1 January 1923) the Southern Railway inherited the following engines that the LBSCR had named after towns, villages, etc, in the area covered by this book.

Class	Type	No	Name	Built	Withdrawn
'D1'	0-4-2T	249	Hilsea	1881	1938
		254	Hambledon	1882	1940
		258	Cosham	1882	1926
		264	Langston	1882	1926
'B1'	0-4-2	174	Fratton	1890	1930
		175	Hayling	1890	1926
		177	Southsea	1890	1927
'D3'	0-4-4T	382	Farlington	1893	1934
		385	Portsmouth	1894	1953
		391	Drayton	1894	1952
'E3'	0-6-2T	169	Bedhampton	1894	1955
'E4'	0-6-2T	506	Catherington	1900	1961
		515	Swanmore	1901	1961
		518	Portchester	1901	1955
		582	Horndean	1903	1956

B.R. 32956

BRITISH RAILWAYS SOUTHERN REGION

MOTIVE POWER DEPARTMENT

STAFF LOANED TO OTHER DEPOTS

DEPOT .... DATE ....

NAME .... GRADE ....

TIME ON DUTY ....

Travel passenger by :

From .... To ....

To Work as .... At .... Depot

Signature of Running Foreman at Receiving

Depot .... Time .... Date ....

If a FIREMAN, name of **Driver** working with and his time on duty ....

Travelled home passenger by .... Train

Signed off duty ....

A copy of this Form is to be handed to all Staff sent to work at a Depot away from their Home Station, and must be retained by him, and returned to the person in charge, after completion of duty.

Signature ....

Grade ....

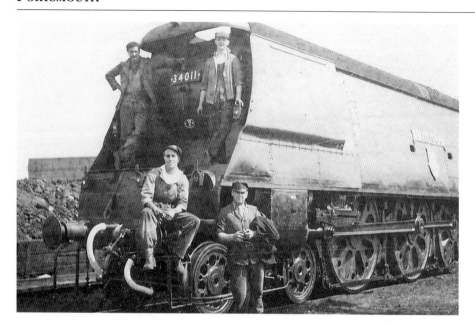

One for the album! 'West Country' Class 4-6-2 No 34011 *Tavistock* is pictured in the late 1950s with some local railwaymen posing for the camera in Fratton yard. Top left is Peter Keeling; top right, Bill Anderson; bottom left, Fred Bristow; and bottom right, Joe Robinson. *Pat Anderson collection*

Also pictured in the late 1950s, alongside the pits in the depot yard, is Marsh Class 'C2X' 0-6-0 No 32548, bearing a 70F (Fratton) shedplate. Prior to 1948 Fratton's code was 'FRA', and from 1948 to the mid-1950s it was 71D. Three Class 'C2X' locomotives were shedded at Fratton during its final years, and they proved to be very versatile engines; apart from being used between Fareham and Portsmouth on the local portion of the Brighton cross-country trains, they were very popular with Fratton drivers who found them very strong for their size. Primarily they were used on freight duties, mostly on the Central section. *John Harris*

Fratton's roundhouse contained a 50-foot turntable, and in June 1963 Standard Class '4' 2-6-0 No 76009 is being turned. Larger locomotives would turn on the triangular system of lines that bordered the depot. *Eric Grace*

Stroudley Class 'A1X' 0-6-0 tank No 32650 is carrying a 71A (Eastleigh) shedplate, since in the early 1960s Fratton no longer had its own code or allocation of locomotives. The Fratton depot staff were very proud of their 'Terriers', and they were always well maintained. They had an association with the depot going back to the 1890s and, apart from their well-known exploits on the Hayling Island branch, were also used on the East Southsea, Lee-on-the-Solent and Bishops Waltham branches. Following a spell on the Isle of Wight between 1930 and 1936, No 32650 became Service locomotive No 515S in 1937, and was used as works pilot at Lancing Carriage & Wagon Works, where in 1946 it was converted to oil-burning for approximately one year. Renumbered 32650, it found its way back to Fratton in 1953. *Eric Grace*

An exceptionally rare arrival at Fratton depot in the summer of 1963 was GWR 'Castle' Class 4-6-0 No 5050 *Earl of St Germans*, which arrived on a special from Bristol. This class was supposedly prohibited from the Portsmouth area, and No 5050 had possibly made slight contact with a platform edge at Fareham en route. The engine was 'impounded' at Fratton depot for almost a month before being allowed to return to Bristol - a 10 mph speed restriction was imposed between Portsmouth and Salisbury! (The full story is recounted in Volume 2 of *Diary of a Train-spotter*.) In this picture No 5050 has only just arrived on shed and is still in steam. *Eric Grace*

Above right A young train-spotter checks his Ian Allan 'ABC' to see what this strange new form of motive power is 'on shed' at Fratton! It is, in fact, a 'Western' Type 4 diesel-hydraulic, which has brought an excursion into Portsmouth Harbour station from the Western Region. *Eric Grace*

Right At the rear of Fratton depot there was a hoist used for lifting locomotives that required repairs that did not necessitate a visit to the locomotive repair shops at Eastleigh. Here 'Terrier' 0-6-0 tank No 32636 is undergoing work, while to the right can be seen one of Maunsell's Class 'S15' 4-6-0s No 30847. Both locomotives were reunited some years later since they managed to avoid the cutter's torch by being purchased for preservation and today reside on the Bluebell Railway in Sussex. *Bruce Oliver*

Left By 1964 Fratton no longer had its own allocation of locomotives and consequently there was plenty of spare room at the depot. Accordingly several historically important steam locomotives earmarked for a place in The National Collection were sent to Fratton for storage. Ultimately they were all stabled within the roundhouse, but pictured outside on 5 April 1964 are Maunsell Class 'N15' 4-6-0 No 30777 Sir *Lamiel* and Class 'LN' 4-6-0 No 30850 *Lord Nelson*. Both locomotives have had a very active 'second life' on the main line in the years following the withdrawal of steam on British Railways in 1968. *Eric Grace*

Below left On the following day, 6 April 1964, towards the end of steam at Fratton, Standard Class '4' 2-6-4T No 80017 receives coal from the crane (DS 200) prior to its return working on the 4.27 pm Portsmouth & Southsea Low Level empty carriages and parcels train to Brighton. *Eric Grace*

With the heavy withdrawal programme of BR steam locomotives in the mid-1960s, Eastleigh Locomotive Works took on the repair of locomotives for other regions of British Railways. Pictured at the rear of Fratton depot in 1965 is LMS Ivatt-designed Class '4' 2-6-0 No 43088 - clearly in 'ex-works' condition. *Eric Grace*

Above 'Britannia' Class locomotives were very infrequent visitors to Portsmouth. Just arrived at Fratton depot on 4 October 1964 is No 70000 *Britannia* (of 5A, Crewe North depot), which is being serviced prior to its return on the Locomotive Club of Great Britain's 'Vectis' tour from Waterloo. Pictured alongside is Standard Class '5' 4-6-0 No 73022. *Eric Grace*

Below Another rare visitor to Fratton was Standard Class '9F' 2-10-0 freight locomotive No 92239, one of a batch allocated to nearby Eastleigh depot towards the end of steam. *Eric Grace*

Promotion at last? Pictured looking after the Fratton depot Foreman's Office is 'Jumbo' Collis, long-time coaling crane operator at the depot. *R. Leovold*

Below An aerial view of Fratton depot yard in early 1967 looking east towards the goods yard sidings. In the foreground is 0-6-0 diesel shunter No 15232 partly obscuring rebuilt 'West Country' Class 'Pacific' No 34047 *Callington.* Of interest in the background is the depot's water tower, the lines of assorted wagons and vans in the goods yard, and the remains of the 'bulging chimney' at St Mary's General Hospital, which for many years was a part of the Fratton scene. The water tower had other uses - on Saturday afternoons, when 'Pompey' were playing at nearby Fratton Park, it would be commonplace to see a line of railwaymen perched on top of the water tower observing the football match - it was obviously a grandstand view! When required for their respective duties, an engine whistle would be blasted three times! *Brian Moss*

Above It's Christmas Day 1966 in Fratton depot roundhouse, but local railway enthusiast John Jones is not in good spirits as he raises his handkerchief to mop away the tears he is shedding as he realises that steam is almost finished here! The solitary steam locomotive is Standard Class '4' 2-6-4T No 80152. *Bruce Oliver*

Below A general view from Fratton station footbridge, looking past the carriage washing unit to the electric multiple unit depot that is responsible for all maintenance of Portsmouth's electric unit trains. The former steam locomotive depot was situated to the left of this view. *Bruce Oliver*

4.
NAVAL ESTABLISHMENTS

The importance of Portsmouth as a naval port covers a span of many centuries and is well chronicled. However, the railway systems at Portsmouth Dockyard and across the harbour at Gosport have always been something of a mystery to most railway enthusiasts. In fact, unless you were in the armed forces or a Dockyard employee, your knowledge would probably have been restricted to seeing BR freight trains entering the yards through guarded gates. How many local railway enthusiasts ever realised that there were over 25 miles of standard gauge track behind the Dockyard walls?

Over the years various different installations sprang up - apart from the Royal Naval Dockyard, there were also separate systems at HMS *Vernon* (Gunwharf) and HMS *Excellent* (Whale Island) adjoining Portsea Island, while at Gosport there were the Priddy's Hard, Bedenham and Frater Depots in addition to the Victualling Depot at Clarence Yard.

Early records depict the existence of wooden tracks in the Dockyard in the 16th century, used primarily to transport heavy ships' masts. Also apparent is the fact that a tramway was laid down during the period 1820-30 with motive power being provided by horses and convicts.

In 1857, ten years after the arrival of the railway in Portsmouth, the first link was built from the main line to the Dockyard. At this time the terminus at Portsmouth was little more than a single platform, but a single-track branch line was created that crossed Union Road (later renamed Commercial Road) at ground level before swinging round into Edinburgh Road prior to entering the Dockyard adjacent to Unicorn Gate. At this date horses were still being used.

The idea of a branch line into the Dockyard had first been raised around the time that the bills authorising the construction of the railway into Portsmouth were put before the House of Commons, but it was rejected because of the inflammable nature of the bulk of the stores kept there. However, by the middle of the 1860s steam traction was in use in the Dockyard, albeit owned by contractors who were constructing Whale Island. It is believed that the Dockyard purchased some of these locomotives before ordering new engines from Manning Wardle in 1871.

In 1876, when the main line was extended from Portsmouth station to Portsmouth Harbour, the High Level platforms were created and the opportunity was taken to create a replacement link into the Dockyard by means of a new line leaving the High Level tracks and passing behind Victoria Park before linking up with the original route at Edinburgh Road. This enabled the previous link, wholly at ground level, to be abandoned. When the military authorities gave permission for the town's defences to be breached to allow construction of the Portsmouth Harbour Extension, two conditions were imposed - the provision of two new access lines, one to Gunwharf (on the south side of the Harbour station) and the other the Watering Island Line Extension.

HMS *Vernon* (Gunwharf)

This single-track railway, now severed, ran down a steep gradient from the city end of the south side of Portsmouth Harbour terminus platforms and into HMS *Vernon* until it reached a point near the main gates. Having reached this point, the track doubled back into the Gunwharf area and there were at least six short sidings leading off to the dockside. The railway was built to transport guns, gun barrels and stores to and from the 25-acre site. Trains needed to reverse out of the station to gain access to the Gunwharf Sidings. The system was taken out of use in 1930, but was re-instated in 1937. The line was decommissioned in 1962.

The current proposed Light Rapid Transport system (LRT) may have plans to route its tracks through part of this area as part of the Millennium programme for improved links with public transport in Portsmouth.

It is also hoped that when the Royal Yacht *Britannia*

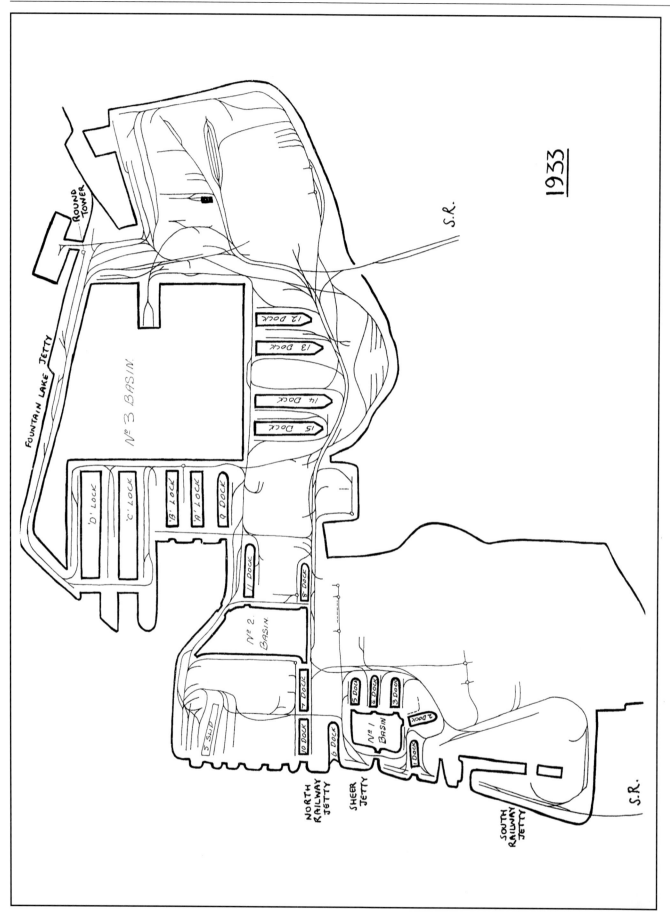

A hand-drawn diagram of the railway system within the Dockyard in 1933. By kind permission of the Dockyard Historical Trust.

An aerial view of Portsmouth Royal Naval Dockyard taken in 1959, and showing roughly the same area as in the diagram. Portsmouth Harbour railway station is in the centre foreground with a local ferry boat moored at the end, and immediately above this is the Watering Island Line, which branched off from the Harbour station and on to the South Railway Jetty where the Victorian 'train shed' can just be seen to the right of the nearest aircraft carrier. In the bottom right-hand corner is one of the tall chimneys of Portsmouth Electricity Power Station, now demolished. This view depicts no fewer than six aircraft carriers, of which three are HMS *Centaur*, HMS *Leviathan* and HMS *Victorious*. *By kind permission of the Dockyard Historical Trust*

has finally ended its days at sea, it will be on public display at the Gunwharf Dock.

The Watering Island Line

Opened in 1878, the Watering Island Line left the main line just before the start of Portsmouth Harbour station's up platforms, and led into the Dockyard via the South Railway Jetty, where an elaborate cast-iron shelter was erected in 1883 - this 'train shed' still stands today, having been fully restored to all its former Victorian glory. The South Railway Jetty (also known as 'Farewell Jetty') was an ideal point, especially during wartime, for troops to embark or disembark from the adjacent moored vessels. Royalty and other VIPs also used this railway line, and today the 'train shed' is still used today to accommodate the Royal limousines when they bring Royalty to this area to board the Royal Yacht. The last Royal Train to use the shed did so in 1939.

The Watering Island Line had a swing bridge that allowed ships to pass through a deep-water channel and moor at The Hard, near the point where today the former HMS *Warrior* is berthed.

Weren't hats popular in days gone by? The launch of HMS *Neptune* in September 1909 has attracted a huge crowd. *By kind permission of the Dockyard Historical Trust*

The line closed soon after the Second World War, the viaduct being in need of urgent repairs, but its complete demolition did not take place until 1960 - prior to this date railway carriages were stored on the line. Today the only remnants of the line are a few wooden supports jutting out of the sea directly opposite the entrance to Portsmouth Harbour station.

With this link removed, a series of tests were carried out on 20 November 1960 over the North Dockyard branch line from Portsmouth & Southsea High Level using Bulleid 'Pacific' main-line steam locomotives Nos 34039 *Boscastle* and 34075 *264 Squadron*, together with Pullman carriages 'Niobe' and 'Cassandra', Royal Saloon 396 and two BR corridor coaches. The tests (probably weight tests) were successful, although they did not lead to the eventual use of this route by Royalty.

Returning now to the railway system within the Dockyard, according to *Trident* (the Naval Base's own newspaper), during its lifetime the railway used 60 steam locomotives and 13 diesels. They had their own engine shed and all necessary repairs were carried out within the Dockyard - there was even a separate shed for the sole passenger carriage that the Dockyard owned (used by the Admiral Superintendent for inspections and special events).

The first diesel locomotives were used during the Second World War, but it was not until 1962 that they totally replaced steam locomotives. Even then two steam engines were held 'in reserve', and one of these subsequently became a mobile boiler supplying steam to the aircraft carrier HMS *Hermes* during a refit. This particular locomotive, No 17, was not scrapped until 1972.

British Railways locomotives, mostly in the form of small steam tank designs (until replaced by 0-6-0 diesel shunters), were regular visitors on account of the daily goods train from Fratton - a service that peaked at 10,000 wagons per year during the Second World War, only to decline to fewer than 700 wagons at the end. The decline had started in the late 1950s - warship-building had ceased, the Royal Navy was being rationalised and road transport, in the form of increasingly effective HGVs, was becoming more and more attractive on the grounds of flexibility. The rail operations within the Dockyard were

gradually scaled down and, with the local Corporation unwilling to contribute towards maintaining the link from High Level to the Dockyard, the final BR goods train ran on 30 November 1977, with the line being finally taken out of use on 5 December 1978.

Today very little remains to provide the casual onlooker with an impression of the previously extensive system that once existed. Parts of the level crossing gates at both Edinburgh Road and Unicorn Gate are still in existence (the Alfred Road crossing gates have been obliterated by road development), and three former goods vehicles (from Bedenham, Gosport) are displayed on a short length of railway track just inside the main Dockyard gate. Away from the city, other items from the railway still exist - wagons have found new homes at the Mid-Hants Railway, Avon Valley Railway and the Somerset & Dorset Trust. In addition, 30 tons of ex-Dockyard railway track were given to the East Somerset Railway.

Above This unfortunate mishap on the Watering Island Line happened in the early 1900s when part of the viaduct structure, the swing bridge, collapsed into the sea, taking with it LBSCR luggage van No 100! *By kind permission of the Dockyard Historical Trust*

Right One of the many 0-4-0 saddle-tank steam locomotives that could once be seen in the Dockyard. This engine, named *Excellent,* was also used at nearby Whale Island. *By kind permission of the Dockyard Historical Trust*

Situated adjacent to the Unicorn Gate entrance of the Royal Naval Dockyard was this single railway platform, seen here in about 1983. Naval ratings boarded the train at this point when going 'on draft' - they would then travel over Alfred Road and Edinburgh Road level crossings, follow the contour of Victoria Park and emerge on to the main line at Portsmouth & Southsea High Level. A maximum of five carriages was imposed on trains using this line. *By kind permission of the Dockyard Historical Trust*

Erected in 1883, the Royal 'train shed' has been fully restored and is still used today by the Royal limousines when Royalty arrive to board the Royal Yacht *Britannia*, which berths alongside. *By kind permission of the Dockyard Historical Trust*

This 1996 view shows some typical restored wagons and vans that were used in the Dockyard, although these three actually finished their working days at the Bedenham Depot in Gosport. During its history the Dockyard owned over 750 wagons, which were used to transport ships' stores, equipment and building materials within the Yard. *Michael G. Harvey*

On 3 November 1963 the Railway Correspondence & Travel Society ran the 'Hayling Island Farewell' tour, which also visited the Portsmouth Dockyard branch. Here Maunsell Class 'U' 2-6-0 No 31791 is pictured between Edinburgh Road and Unicorn Gate crossings. *Bruce Oliver*

Bulleid 'Pacific' No 34088 *213 Squadron* leads the rail tour of 3 November 1963 through Edinburgh Road crossing gates from the High Level platforms at Portsmouth & Southsea station. Today a plaque displayed on the one remaining gate reads: 'This gate and posts are relics of the Dockyard Railway link that used to pass over Edinburgh Road. The track was completed in 1846 [*sic*] and used until 1977. The line was dismantled during the 1980s to allow for landscaping along Unicorn Road.' *Bruce Oliver*

Another view of No 34088 on the same occasion, leaving the North Dockyard line and passing the High Level signal box at Portsmouth & Southsea station. *Bruce Oliver*

HMS *Excellent* Railway (Whale Island)

Today many Portsmouth citizens know Whale Island as a naval base sited just off the Rudmore area of the city and joined by a road bridge, but very few people realise that at one time it had its own railway system, known as the *Excellent* Railway.

In 1864, when enormous amounts of spoil from Portsmouth Royal Naval Dockyard were being disposed of (due to large-scale extension works in that area), it was decided to build a viaduct from the Dockyard across Fountain Lake to dump this spoil, and this location was originally called 'Big Whale Island'. Convicts were used to assist in the construction of the viaduct and for the dumping of the spoil. Adjoining this island were exposed mud flats, and these were known as 'Little Whale Island'. Eventually the Admiralty bought the land and it was extended to become one island, known as Whale Island from its shape. This became the base of HMS *Excellent*.

The viaduct was demolished in 1895 when the last load of spoil had been brought over. However, the rail system, which by this time ran around the island, was kept to allow the movement of heavy equipment such as guns and stores to the various sections.

A road system was still difficult to construct because of the settling mud. The exact date of the demise of the railway is not too clear, but roads were laid in the 1920s around the island, many of which were constructed over the former railway, which by all accounts was of standard gauge, although some records suggest that a 15-inch or a 2-foot gauge could have been used. By the 1930s very little of the railway system existed; what was left was mainly located on the south-west corner of the island.

The railway was always in tremendous demand for children's parties (see the accompanying photograph). The island once had its own zoo, and among its animals were bears and lions; the children's parties no doubt included a visit.

In 1919, when there was a threat of a national rail strike, the Whale Island Railway was used to train selected officers and ratings in the duties of train crews. However, much to the regret of those trained, they were never called upon!

We acknowledge the kind assistance of Lt Cdr Brian Witts MBE (Rtd) for the above information and for the use of photographs.

The viaduct from the Dockyard to Whale Island, showing the swing bridge, which allowed ships into Fountain Lake. On the extreme right is the steam locomotive hauling its wagons loaded full of spoil. *By courtesy of Brian Witts*

Happy days at HMS *Excellent*! A train-load of children (well supervised by naval staff) take a ride in open wagons decorated with flags in about 1900 - such children's parties were much in demand. Behind the steam engine is a very smart four-wheeled carriage, beautifully turned out for the occasion, as is the 0-4-0 saddle-tank. *By courtesy of Brian Witts*

Dockyard railway excursions

In the 19th century the Dockyard was the biggest employer in the area, and various social functions were arranged for the workers and their families.

The first recorded railway excursion was arranged in conjunction with the LBSCR on 22 September 1883. Following the success of this innovation the Portsmouth Dockyard Excursion Committee was formed and the first official excursion was arranged to the Fisheries Exhibition in London the following month. This proved very popular, with 671 of the 700 available tickets being sold. To celebrate the Queen's Birthday, traditionally a Dockyard holiday, the next excursion was run on 24 May 1884, and a copy of the handbill advertising the event is included below.

In those days, before the advent of the motor car, these railway excursions were exceptionally popular, as is evidenced by the constantly increasing passenger figures - in 1886, 6,708 passengers were carried, while ten years later this had increased to 30,604, before peaking at a remarkable 38,478 in 1908! The majority of the excursions were run to coincide with the monarch's birthdays and Bank Holidays, but football specials and visits to London Exhibitions were also well supported.

Unfortunately the 1914-18 war eventually put a stop to these excursions (see the letter reproduced overleaf), and even after the war the railway companies were loath to provide the previous facilities, preferring instead to add extra coaches to normal service trains. Passenger figures never again attained the volumes seen prior to the war, and although the excursions to the British Empire Exhibitions in 1924 and 1925 were well attended, the General Strike of 1926 had a drastic effect, and thereafter the excursion traffic rapidly declined before being discontinued in 1935.

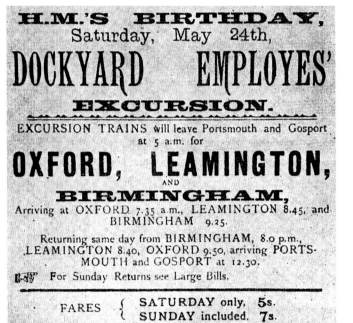

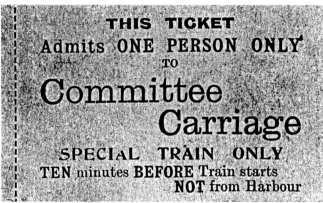

Left A handbill advertising a Dockyard employees' excursion from Portsmouth and Gosport to Oxford, Leamington and Birmingham on 24 May 1884. *Charles Kemp collection*

Above A ticket for the Committee Carriage. *Charles Kemp collection*

Below Timings and other details for an excursion to Winchester. *Charles Kemp collection*

DOCKYARD EXCURSION, PORTSMOUTH TO WINCHESTER.

Special trains will run as under :—

No. 201.

	ARR. P.M.	DEP. P.M.
Portsmouth ...	...	1 0
Fratton ...	1 2	1 3
Portcreek Jct. ...		1 8
Cosham Jct. ...		1 10
Fareham ...	1 20	1 21
Swanwick ...		1 28
Netley ...	1 35	1 36
Woolston ...		1 41
St. Denys ...		1 46
Northam ...	1 49	1 52
Southampton ...	1 55	2 2
Winchester ...	2 28	...

Fratton Loco. to provide engine.

Portsmouth to provide train,— including as many lavatory thirds as possible.

Inspector Kirk, guard.

Passengers may be allowed to return from Netley by the 8.9 p.m. ordinary train.

(B. 2/213,524.) (N. 41,392.)

No. 202.

	ARR. P.M.	DEP. P.M.
Winchester ...	...	9 5
Southampton ...	9 24	9 40
Northam ...		9 42
St. Denys ...		9 45
Woolston ...		9 51
Netley ...	9 57	10 0
Swanwick ...		10 7
Fareham ...	10 14	10 16
Cosham Jct. ...		10 26
Portcreek Jct. ...		10 28
Fratton ...	10 33	10 35
Portsmouth Tn.	10 38	...

Joint South Western and Brighton Committee.

Superintendent's Office,

Portsmouth Town Station

RETURN EXCURSIONS FROM PORTSMOUTH, SATURDAY, 7th JULY, 1906.

Departure time. Harbour.	Town.	Destination.	Description.	Platform.
p.m.	p.m.			
	6.0	Waterloo	Ordinary	4
	6.15	Southampton	,,	3
6.25	6.30	Brighton	,,	High Level
	6.58	Eastleigh	,,	1
7.0	7.6	Waterloo	,,	High Level
7.5	7.10	Victoria	Excursion	High Level
	7.15	Waterloo	Ordinary	3
7.15	7.20	Victoria	,,	High Level
7.20	7.25	London Bridge	,,	High Level
	7.30	Avonmouth, G.W.	Excursion	
7.30	7.35	Tunbridge Wells	,,	High Level
7.50	7.58	Waterloo	,,	High Level
7.50	7.55	London Bridge	,,	High Level
7.57	8.2	Victoria	,,	High Level
8.0	8.5	Reading, G.W.	,,	High Level
	8.10	Croydon	,,	3
	8.15	,,	,,	4
	8.15	Trowbridge, G.W.	,,	2
8.20	8.25	Waterloo	,,	High Level
	8.30	Bristol, G.W.	,,	5
	8.35	Staines	,,	3
	8.40	Eastleigh	Ordinary	2
	8.45	Staines	Excursion	4
8.40	8.45	Coventry, L.&.N.W.	,,	High Level
8.45	8.50	Waterloo	Ordinary	High Level
	9.0	Brighton	,,	1
	9.5	,,	Relief	2
	9.10	Southampton	Ordinary	1
	9.20	Bristol, G.W.	Excursion	3
9.20	9.25	Hitchin, G.N.	,,	High Level
	9.30	Bristol, G.W.	,,	4
9.30	9.35	Hitchin, G.N.	,,	High Level
	9.40	Wolverhampton, G.W.	,,	3
	9.45	,,	,,	4
	9.55	Walsall, Mid.	,,	High Level
10.5	10.10	Watford, L.&.N.W.	,,	High Level
	10.15	Wolverhampton, G.W.	,,	3
10.20	10.25	Coventry, L.&.N.W.	,,	High Level
	10.35	Birmingham, Mid.	,,	3
	10.45	Eastleigh	Ordinary	1
	11.5	Yeovil	Excursion	4
11.0	11.10	Exeter	,,	High Level
	11.10	Chichester	Ordinary	1
11.5	11.15	Crediton	Excursion	High Level
	11.20	Yeovil	,,	3
	11.25	Fareham	Ordinary	1

—————— R.W.M. ——————

London, Brighton & South Coast Railway.

EED.

Office of Superintendent of the Line,

London Bridge Station, S.E.

TELEGRAPHIC ADDRESS,
OASTSUP, RAIL, LONDON
TELEPHONE No.1355 Hop.
4763

In your reply please quote this reference

16th February, 1915.

E.1.Pad.18.Q.

Dear Sir,

TRIPS TO LONDON. FEBRUARY 27TH & MARCH 18TH, 1915.

I regret to inform you that in consequence of the imperative requirements of the Military Authorities, it has been found necessary to cancel all Day and Half-day Excursion facilities on and from Monday next the 22nd instant.

I will advise you in due course when normal working is resumed.

Yours faithfully,

Finlay Scott,

per

C. Milne Esqre.,
   164 Chichester Road,
      North End,
         PORTSMOUTH..HANTS.

Above An official letter from the LBSCR dated 16 February 1915 informing of the cancellation of excursions owing to the outbreak of war. *Charles Kemp collection*

Left Just look at the destinations and volume of return rail excursion traffic from Portsmouth on Saturday 7 July 1906! *Charles Kemp collection*

Priddy's Hard, Bedenham and Frater

The systems across Portsmouth Harbour at Gosport managed to survive a little longer. The Royal Navy had built an extensive rail system within the establishments at Priddy's Hard, Bedenham and Frater, primarily for the transport of munitions. The first railway is believed to have started up in the mid-1800s and was of a narrow gauge. Within 50 years there were two manually operated lines of 1 ft 6 in and 2 ft 6 in gauges, the latter eventually displacing the smaller one. Lines within these establishments were worked by Battery Rail Tractors until 1960, when Road Tractor Units took over, resulting in the closure of the line.

A standard gauge (4 ft 8½ in) system was opened with-in these establishments in 1912. Prior to total closure in the early 1990s a plentiful selection of motive power was used, the majority being 'fireless' locomotives and diesels. An exception was an 0-4-0 saddle-tank steam locomotive fitted with a large spark-arrestor chimney, which was necessary as stringent precautions had to be taken owing to the fire risk associated with the transport of munitions. There is evidence of a locomotive being bought from the LSWR, and ex-BR fireman George Blakey distinctly recollects working there on Class 'A1X' 0-6-0 'Terrier' tanks - two were spare at Fratton depot during and just after the Second World War.

Today there are countless reminders of the previous existence of the railway system at Gosport, with former level crossing gates (still regularly painted) a common feature of the back streets.

5.
GOODS YARDS AND SIDINGS

In September 1929 the 2.38 pm train to Reading leaves Portsmouth High Level behind a GWR Class '4300' 2-6-0 locomotive. To the far right of the picture can be seen the tracks leading into the goods sidings (including the Fish Dock) and the Low Level platforms, while behind the water tower in the centre of the picture is the goods shed.

This large building was erected within a few years of the railway's arrival and was served by extensive sidings (originally used solely by the LSWR); these ran alongside Greetham Street, which in those days still had tracks for the use of trams. The goods shed was replaced in July 1936 by a new facility at Fratton. *Alf Coffin*

Early memories and my work on the railway

by George Lee

From 1935 my father worked for Chaplins, which were agents for the Southern Railway and delivered most of the goods that came in by rail to the goods shed, which was under Portsmouth High Level. This shed was approached via a pair of large double gates directly opposite the Guildhall. As a lad I used to assist my father at this location.

In the summer months the Town station was absolutely packed with 'PLA' (Passengers' Luggage in Advance); this basically was luggage sent from *any* location on Britain's railways to Portsmouth in advance of the passenger, and no matter what the distance the cost in the 1935/6 period was a fixed 1 shilling. I recall the station clock being practically obscured by mountains of luggage!

Leading into the station from what was then Station Street was an alley known locally as 'Chippy Chase', where the lorries backed in to load the PLA - all this was located near the passenger entrance to the station. Also, off Station Street, just past the alley, were two sizeable wooden gates that gave access to the station. A platform was near here, and further along, on the opposite side, was the 'Fish Dock' - named because there was a fish train that arrived every morning direct from Grimsby. All the Portsmouth area fish merchants would congregate here between 4.30 am and 5 am to pick up their quota of fish.

One regular excursion train into Portsmouth was from the 'Black Cat' cigarette factory, laid on for the factory workers. When they arrived they stayed 'under canvas' on Southsea Common near the popular walkway known as 'Ladies' Mile'.

As a point of interest, the old goods shed at the Town station was re-sited at Fratton about 1936, adjacent to Goldsmith Avenue and close to Fratton Park.

I started work on the railway in March 1943 as an 'oiler boy' with the Carriage & Wagon Department at Portsmouth Town station; from there I was upgraded to 'adult oiler' and then to 'repairer' - this entailed work on wagons at Fratton. My duties then took me to the title of 'Carriage & Wagon Examiner', and this included examining and checking all parts of electric units and steam stock, including lighting, steam heating, brake adjusting, wheels and wheel flanges - there was always something to check out and leisure-time was minimal!

Although I've referred to it as Portsmouth Town station, it was in fact renamed Portsmouth & Southsea as far back as 1921. It had five low-level platforms. Just past the 'Fish Dock' was a large lock-up cage, known as the 'Monkey House' - opposite this were our cabins, mess room and store room.

Prior to the new power signal box being installed at the

Town station on the Canal Walk side (located directly opposite its predecessor on the Greetham Street side), the roads at the top of the station were named the 'third road' for berthing carriages; on the opposite side was the DCS (Down Carriage Sidings), which were later altered to allow electric unit stock to use them.

Fratton was mainly for goods work, but it also berthed quite a sizeable amount of steam stock in what was known as the 'Field Sidings', which were next to the large goods shed and adjacent to Fratton Park.

The carriage shed, adjacent to Goldsmith Avenue, was also a cleaning shed and in later years had two roads for maintenance work. The old yard was known mostly for its coal roads; many of the local coal merchants used to go there and shovel and bag their own coal directly out of the open-sided rail wagons! One job that particularly stands out in my memory was when the coal wagons were 'pushed' by an engine from these roads at Fratton down to the DCS at the Town station (about 20 wagons in all) - these were for Portsmouth Electricity Power Station at Old Portsmouth. The shunter used to sit up on top of the loaded coal wagon, leading with his red and green flags; he would wave to the driver and away they would go; I don't think this practice would be tolerated in today's world!

Fratton had quite a number of goods and parcel trains in and out of the yard daily. I used to work into the Royal Naval Dockyard branch (Monday to Friday) from Fratton - the first train into the yard was at 9.30 am and out at 11.30 am, then back again at 2 pm and out at 4.20 pm. The goods train departed from Fratton reception road, up the high level at the Town station until we 'cleared' the platform; then we backed on to the opposite platform until we were clear of the points, then forward down past Victoria Park, across Edinburgh Road and Alfred Road level crossings, entering the Dockyard via the Unicorn Gate level crossing. On this turn it was my job to examine the 'in' and 'out' goods wagons; occasionally we had a 'Gun Carriage' which was used to carry large 12-inch guns off the battleships berthed in the Dockyard - these would be en route for maintenance.

Portsmouth Harbour station in the heyday of the 1950s and 1960s was often packed solid with holidaymakers going to the Isle of Wight, especially on Bank Holidays and midsummer weekends. I remember that when passengers alighted from their respective excursion carriages they had to line up from the top ends of the platforms to wait for the boats to Ryde (this service was continual during the summer service). I have known crowds lined up from the Harbour platforms as far round as HMS *Vernon* - over 300 yards away!

In those early days the vessels were owned by the Southern Railway and paddle-steamers were still in use. Often when off-loading their passengers the weight would be totally on one side and consequently one could see one of the paddles out of the water!

In the mid-1980s substantial rebuilding took place at Portsmouth & Southsea station, as this February 1985 photograph shows. Some Low Level platforms were removed, as were all the sidings on the north side of the station (right-hand side of the photograph) in order to create room for a car park and DIY store, replaced in 1997 by a cut-price warehouse. *Bruce Oliver*

One of the earliest third rail electric units used on the Southern Railway is pictured in Fratton sidings in 1960 in its final form. Originally built as '3SUB' No 1782, it was augmented to a four-car unit after the Second World War and renumbered as '4SUB' No 4579. When withdrawn from service in 1953 it was reduced to its original three coaches, stripped of its seating, etc, and fitted out internally as a mobile classroom. It re-entered traffic in April 1956 as Departmental unit No S10 and was eventually withdrawn in 1974, having earlier been renumbered, yet again, to 053. *Bruce Oliver*

In August 1991 many Class 456 units were stored, pending modifications, in the sidings at Fratton - seen here alongside an ex-London Transport underground unit, returned from the Isle of Wight. The sidings on which these units stand were the first installed by the LBSCR and were in place by the 1880s. Dominating the background is the goods shed opened in July 1936, and at that time one of the largest in Great Britain with a length of 500 feet and a width of 135 feet. This building survived until December 1995, when it was demolished. Fratton motive power depot was situated between the stored units and the goods shed. *Bruce Oliver*

By the 1980s Fratton goods sidings were little used other than for storage of redundant electric units, and this August 1981 view finds '4SUB' unit No 4693 stored alongside the goods shed. *Bruce Oliver*

When Fratton goods shed was opened in 1936, further sidings were built alongside the 'Football Lanes' leading to Fratton Park Football Club ground. When these were no longer needed, they too were used for storage purposes, as this July 1984 picture of stored '2HAP' units shows. *Bruce Oliver*

This May 1986 photograph, with the electric unit depot forming the background, shows a Class 33 diesel locomotive hauling empty carriages out of Fratton yard. A Service unit, No 023, formerly a '2HAL' unit, can be seen on the left. *Bruce Oliver*

This '2BIL' electric unit, No 2121, was badly damaged in a collision at Portsmouth Harbour station, and as a result was scrapped at Fratton goods yard sidings in the late 1960s. *Colin Saunders*

May 1984 brought an exceptionally unusual visitor to Fratton goods yard in the form of this 'SPENO' Rail Grinder. It was used to re-profile the tracks, which involved the removal of corrugations. *Bruce Oliver*

In May 1978 a Class 31 locomotive is seen approaching Hilsea station on a service from the Western Region; note that the train has six vehicles and that the full brake is within the set. On the left of the picture is the site of the former government sidings and military buildings. In the background can be seen the Hilsea Lines, military defences dating from the 19th century, which the railway breached with a very short 'tunnel'. On the right of the picture a Portsmouth Corporation Atlantean is standing alongside the GEC Marconi factory, awaiting customers. Hilsea station opened in 1941 to serve the military and industrial facilities. *Bruce Oliver*

Above Beyer Peacock 0-4-0 saddle-tank locomotive No 2 *Farlington* is pictured at Hilsea Gas Works, Portsmouth, with its proud driver alongside. When this photograph was taken in July 1961 diesel traction was already in use at this location. The engines had their own small one-road shed alongside the main line. *Bruce Oliver*

Below No 1398 *Lord Fisher*, an 0-4-0 saddle-tank, was built in 1915 by Andrew Barclay of Kilmarnock and initially worked at the Royal Naval Aircraft Station at Kingsnorth, Kent, before moving on to the Royal Aircraft Establishment at Farnborough, Hampshire, until 1939, when it was employed at RAF Cardington in Yorkshire. In 1942 it was sold to Yorktown (Camberley) & District Gas & Electricity Company in Surrey, before yet another transfer to Blackwater Gas Works in 1949, where it worked until

displaced by a more powerful locomotive. Now in need of overhaul, in August 1956 it was sent to Portsmouth's Hilsea Gas Works as back-up for its two Beyer Peacock 0-4-0 saddle tanks, *Farlington* and *Sir John Baker*. However, it soon became obvious that its lack of power did not warrant its reconditioning and it was stored out of use in the open, as seen here on 10 June 1960; in November of that year it was moved to Southampton Gas Works, where it was overhauled before being put to work again in 1961 on the Chapel Tramway. When this system closed in 1967 the locomotive was sold to Barry Buckfield for preservation and, following periods at the abortive Longmoor Railway Centre and at the Somerset & Dorset Railway Circle's base at Radstock, it ultimately arrived at Cranmore on the East Somerset Railway, where it has been regularly steamed. *Michael G. Harvey*

Drummond-designed Class 'T9' 4-4-0 No 30283 carries out some shunting duties at Cosham station in the late 1940s. At this time a five-track goods yard existed on the north side of the station complete with a large goods shed, which contained a single track with doors at both ends; it still survives today, without the track, and is used by Erith Building Supplies. This yard also had a small crane on a pivot and a loading gauge. There was a cattle dock and sidings on the south side of the station adjacent to Windsor Road, and the track leading to this can be seen to the middle right of the picture. A single track also ran behind the south-side platform, which was originally used as the terminus for steam push-pull 'motor trains' to and from Havant via the north side of the Cosham triangle. *Denis Callender*

6.
LOST LINES

The Gosport branch

As mentioned at the beginning of this book, in 1841 Gosport attained its railway, before Portsmouth, by means of a branch line built from Bishopstoke (Eastleigh) on the Southampton to London route. However, little over a century later it had the misfortune of being the largest town in the country without a railway passenger service when this facility was withdrawn in 1953.

The line was built at a cost of just over £400,000 and opened on 29 November 1841 (four months behind schedule), only to close four days later on account of a landslip north of Fareham! It was re-opened on 7 February 1842 and, prior to the arrival of the railway in Portsmouth, provided the service to London for the local community. The people of Portsmouth were, of course, inconvenienced by the need to use a ferry to cross Portsmouth Harbour, while the inhabitants of Gosport also suffered to some extent since the station was situated some half a mile away from the town on account of the refusal of the military authority to allow the breaching of the town's fortifications.

Initially there were only the two stations on the branch, Fareham and Gosport (Fort Brockhurst did not open until 1865), but following separate visits by Prince Albert and Queen Victoria in 1844 and the purchase of Osborne House on the Isle of Wight, the LSWR was persuaded to provide a 605-yard extension into Royal Clarence Yard, where a station for the exclusive use of the monarchy was built - sanction to breach the fortifications was this time readily provided. Over the years Queen Victoria made great use of this route to reach the Victualling Yard Pier for transportation to the Isle of Wight. It is widely believed that she was firmly opposed to using the facilities on the other side of the harbour at Portsmouth because of her dislike of that town.

On 2 February 1901 Queen Victoria's funeral train left the Royal Clarence Yard, thus effectively ending the regular royal connection with Gosport since her son gave

Osborne House to the nation shortly afterwards. However, the station remains standing today, albeit in a sad state of repair. It was a very grand affair built at a cost of almost £11,000 to the design of William Tite. It was constructed in the Italian style with elegant columns, much in contrast to Fareham station, which was built at a cost of only £1,392, yet went on to become a major junction, with not only the Gosport branch but also lines to Portsmouth (via Cosham), Southampton (via Netley), Eastleigh (via Botley), and the Meon Valley to Alton.

Gosport appears to have had a two-road brick-built engine shed from the opening of the line in 1841. In 1906, along with Bishops Waltham, it was listed as a sub-shed of Northam (Southampton) in the Southern District of the LSWR. It later became a sub-shed of Fratton, which, in later years, provided motive power such as Class 'M7' 0-4-4 tank locomotives for shunting and Clarence Yard and Meon Valley duties. Gosport engine shed did not have a turntable and engines used the Stokes Bay triangle to turn. The building was partially destroyed in an air attack during the Second World War and was replaced by a single-road corrugated and asbestos structure, which, although closed at the same time as passenger services were withdrawn (1953) and later demolished, was still used as a stabling point until 1962.

At the opening of the Gosport branch line trains to London (Nine Elms) had a journey time of almost 3½ hours, to which of course the inhabitants of Portsmouth had to add further travelling time to make their way across the harbour. It was therefore no surprise that passenger services in Gosport started their decline when the first line to Portsmouth was opened in 1847. The competition increased still further in 1859 when the Portsmouth Direct Line to London (via Haslemere) was opened, and the opening of Portsmouth Harbour station in 1876 deprived the Gosport area of a great deal of the Isle of Wight traffic.

The holiday resorts of Stokes Bay and Lee-on-the-Solent never grew to the extent expected, and the low passenger receipts and competition from the trams forced the early closure of these lines, thereby to some extent reducing the importance of the Gosport branch. Similarly, the arrival of the Meon Valley line was an opportunity wasted since it was never promoted sufficiently well to realise its potential as an alternative route to London. Other ideas floated at various times that might have saved the line included a tunnel to the Isle of Wight from Stokes Bay, the use of a 'Michelin' petrol-driven, rubber-tyred railcar, and electrification.

As a cost-cutting measure the Gosport branch was made a single line in 1934, and although it saw much more activity during the Second World War, as it had during the First World War on account of the local military presence, the passenger service only managed to survive until 6 June 1953. Freight services, which to a large extent had contributed for so long to the survival of the line, continued until 30 January 1969, when the remaining facilities at Gosport station were withdrawn, leaving, for a while longer, freight working between Fareham and the military depot at Bedenham sidings, a brief description of which was provided in the previous chapter.

Today, although ultimately a Rapid Transit System is planned for the future, one cannot help wondering why the line between Fareham and Gosport was not redeveloped over the last two or three decades to combat the horrific road congestion seen daily on the notorious A32 between the two towns.

Businessmen were not slow to miss an opportunity even in the 19th century. *The Hampshire Telegraph* of 14 February 1842 carried the following advertisement at the time of the re-opening of the Gosport line:

LONDON & SOUTHWEST RAILWAY
THE RE-OPENING OF GOSPORT LINE.

An hotel has been built expressly for the ACCOMMODATION of RAILWAY TRAVELLERS, immediately adjoining the Gosport TERMINUS. Well aired BEDS, Breakfasts, Dinners, Lunches and Refreshments of every description are always ready on the arrival and departure of the several trains, and W. J. COCKERILL stands pledged to the Railway Company (whose patronage he has the honour to acknowledge) to moderate charges and to spare no exertions to render his Establishment worthy of support.

N.B. Porters are in attendance for the removal of luggage. FLYS (a LIGHT two seated carriage) are kept on the premises; and Omnibuses to and from all parts of Portsea and Portsmouth every hour during the day.

In June 1951 Drummond Class 'M7' 0-4-4T No 30050 is seen at Fareham at the junction of the Gosport and Portsmouth lines; it is the latter that curves off behind the locomotive since the first 'direct route' was to Gosport. *Denis Callender*

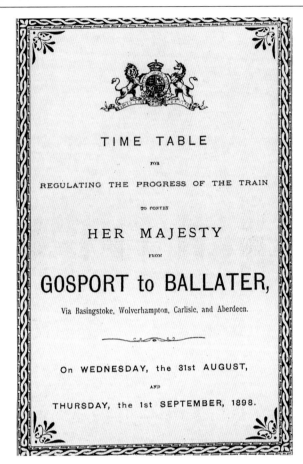

TIME TABLE

FOR

REGULATING THE PROGRESS OF THE TRAIN

TO CONVEY

HER MAJESTY

FROM

GOSPORT to BALLATER,

Via Basingstoke, Wolverhampton, Carlisle, and Aberdeen.

On WEDNESDAY, the 31st AUGUST,

AND

THURSDAY, the 1st SEPTEMBER, 1898.

GOSPORT TO BALLATER.

County.	Gradient.	Distance from Gosport.	Name of Station.	Time Table.	Actual Time.
		Miles.	*[31st Aug., 1898.]*	P.M.	P.M.
Hampshire		...	**Gosport** ... ...dep.	**7 40**	
		⅜	Gosport Station ... „	7 43	
		1⅝	Fort Brockhurst ...pass	7 45	
		5⅛	Fareham ... ... „	7 55	
		10½	Botley ... ... „	8 4	
		16	Eastleigh ... ... „	8 16	
		20½	Shawford Junc. ... „	8 23	
		23	Winchester ... ... „	8 27	
		25	Winchester Junc. „	8 30	
		31⅜	Micheldever ... „	8 40	
		41⅞	**Basingstoke** ... arr.	**8 55**	
			„ ...dep.	**9 0**	
		46⅞	Bramley ... ... pass	9 9	
Berks		50⅛	Mortimer ... ... „	9 14	
		57⅛	Reading (West J.) „	9 27	
		58¾	Tilehurst ... ... „	9 31	
		61⅝	Pangbourne... ... „	9 35	
Oxford		64⅞	Goring & Streatley „	9 39	
Berks		68⅝	Cholsey & Moulsford „	9 43	
		71	Moreton Cutting... „	9 47	
Oxford		73	Didcot ... ... „ (Avoiding Line)	9 51	
		76⅜	Culham... ... ... „	9 56	
Berks		78⅞	Radley ... ... „	9 59	
		81⅛	Kennington Junc. „	10 3	
Oxford		83½	Oxford ... ... „	10 7	
		86¼	Wolvercot Junc. „	10 12	
		89	Kidlington ... ... „	10 16	
		91⅛	Bletchington ... „	10 19	
		95¼	Heyford ... ... „	10 25	
		98⅛	Somerton ... ... „	10 29	
Northampton		100¼	Aynho ... ... „	10 32	
		102½	King's Sutton ... „	10 35	

County.	Gradient.	Distance from Gosport.	Name of Station.	Time Table.	Actual Time.
		Miles.	*[31st Aug., 1898.]*	P.M.	P.M.
Oxford		106½	Banbury ... pass.	10 40	
		109¾	Cropredy ... ... „	10 45	
Warwick		114⅞	Fenny Compton ... „	10 53	
		119⅛	Greaves Siding ... „	11 0	
		119⅞	Southam Road „	11 1	
		126	**Leamington** ... arr.	**11 11**	
			(Refreshments—15 Mins.)		
			„ ... ...dep.	**11 26**	
		127⅞	Warwick ... ... pass	11 29	
		132	Hatton ... ... „	11 35	
		136¼	Kingswood ... ... „	11 42	
		138⅞	Knowle... ... ... „	11 46	
		142¼	Solihull ... ... „	11 51	
		144	Olton ... ... „	11 54	
		145	Acock's Green ... „	11 56	
		147	Small Heath ... „	11 59	
			[1st Sept., 1898.]	A.M.	A.M.
		148	Bordesley ... ... „	12 3	
		149¼	**Birmingham** ... arr.	**12 6**	
			„ ... dep.	**12 11**	
Stafford		152¼	Handsworth Junc. pass	12 17	
		154	West Bromwich ... „	12 20	
		156⅝	Wednesbury ... „	12 26	
		159	Bilston ... ... „	12 30	
		160	Priestfield ... ... „	12 32	
		161⅝	**Wolverhampton** arr.	**12 36**	
			„ dep.	**12 43**	
		163⅛	Bushbury Junction pass	12 47	
		167½	Four Ashes ... ... „	12 56	
		168⅞	Gailey ... ... „	12 59	
		171⅛	Penkridge ... ... „	1 3	
		176¾	Stafford ... ... „	1 12	
		180	Great Bridgeford „	1 17	
		182⅛	Norton Bridge ... „	1 20	
		186⅜	Standon Bridge ... „	1 27	
		190¾	Whitmore ... ... „	1 33	
		193⅜	Madeley ... ... „	1 37	
Cheshire		196½	Betley Road ... „	1 42	
		201⅜	Crewe ... ... „	1 48	
		206⅛	Minshull Vernon „	1 55	
		208¾	Winsford ... ... „	1 58	

GOSPORT TO BALLATER—*Continued.*

County.	Gradient.	Distance from Gosport.	Name of Station.	Time Table.	Actual Time.
		Miles.	*[1st Sept., 1898.]*	A.M.	A.M.
Lanark		423	Braidwood ... ...pass	7 32	
		424¼	Carluke ... ... „	7 34	
		426¼	Law Junction .. „	7 37	
		427⅛	Garriongill ... ... „	7 38	
		428⅞	Wishaw (South) ... „	7 41	
		430	Shieldmuir ... ... „	7 43	
		430⅝	Flemington ... ... „	7 44	
		431⅞	Motherwell ... ... „	7 46	
		433⅞	Mossend ... ... „	7 49	
		436⅞	Whifflet ... ... „	7 53	
		437⅛	Coatbridge ... ... „	7 54	
		438¼	Gartsherrie ... ... „	7 56	
		439	Garnqueen J.(South) „	7 57	
Dumbarton		439½	Glenboig ... ... „	7 58	
		443⅜	Cumbernauld ... „	8 3	
		449	Greenhill ... ... „	8 11	
Stirling		452⅝	Larbert ... ... „	8 16	
		454¾	Alloa Junction ... „	8 19	
		456¾	Plean Junction ... „	8 22	
		458¼	Bannockburn ... „	8 24	
		460⅜	Stirling ... ... „	8 28	
		463⅝	Bridge of Allan ... „	8 32	
Perth		465⅝	Dunblane ... ... „	8 35	
		468¼	Kinbuck ... ... „	8 39	
		471½	**Greenloaning** arr.	**8 43**	
			„ dep.	**8 48**	
		475¾	Blackford ... ... pass	8 54	
		477⅞	Crieff Junction ... „	8 57	
		480	Auchterarder ... „	9 0	
		484⅛	Dunning ... ... „	9 5	
		486⅞	Forteviot ... ... „	9 9	
		489¾	Forgandenny ... „	9 13	
		491⅛	Hilton Junction ... „	9 16	
		493⅛	**Perth** ... . arr.	**9 20**	
			(Refreshments—45 Mins.)		
			Perth ... ... dep.	**10 5**	
		495¾	Almond Valley Jn. pass	10 9	
		497⅛	Luncarty ... ... „	10 13	
		498¾	Strathord ... ... „	10 15	
		500¾	Stanley ... ... „	10 18	
		503⅛	Ballathie ... ... „	10 21	
		505	Cargill ... ... „	10 24	
		507¾	Woodside ... ... „	10 28	
		509½	Coupar Angus ... „	10 31	
		512	Ardler ... ... „	10 34	
Forfar		514¼	Alyth Junction ... „	10 37	
		518⅜	Eassie ... ... „	10 43	
		520¼	Glamis ... ... „	10 46	

County.	Gradient.	Distance from Gosport.	Name of Station.	Time Table.	Actual Time.
		Miles.	*[1st Sept., 1898.]*	A.M.	A.M.
Forfar		523⅜	Kirriemuir Junc. pass	10 50	
		526½	Forfar ... ... „	10 54	
		528½	Clocksbriggs ... „	10 58	
		531⅛	Auldbar Road ... „	11 2	
		533⅛	Guthrie Junction „	11 5	
		535⅛	Glasterlaw ... ... „	11 8	
		538½	Farnell Road ... „	11 13	
		541⅛	Bridge of Dun ... „	11 18	
		544¼	Dubton Junc. ... „	11 22	
		545½	Kinnaber Junc. ... „	11 24	
		547⅜	Craigo ... ... „	11 28	
Kincardine		549¾	Marykirk ... ... „	11 31	
		552⅞	Laurencekirk ... „	11 36	
		556¼	Fordoun ... ... „	11 41	
		560⅛	Drumlithie ... ... „	11 47	
		561⅛	Newmill ... ... „	11 50	
		567⅝	Stonehaven ... ... „	11 58	
				P.M.	P.M.
		572	Muchalls ... ... „	12 7	
		573⅛	Newtonhill ... ... „	12 9	
		575⅛	Portlethen ... ... „	12 13	
		578⅜	Cove ... ... „	12 18	
Aberdeen		582⅞	**Aberdeen**... ... arr.	**12 25**	
			„ ... ... dep.	**12 30**	
		583⅝	Holburn Street ... pass	12 32	
		584	Ruthrieston ... ... „	12 33	
		585¼	Pitfodels ... ... „	12 35	
		585¾	Cults ... ... „	12 36	
		586⅜	West Cults ... ... „	12 37	
		587	Bieldside ... ... „	12 38	
		587⅜	Murtle ... ... „	12 39	
		588¼	Milltimber ... ... „	12 40	
		589¾	Culter ... ... „	12 42	
Kincardine		592	Drum ... ... „	12 46	
		593	Park ... ... „	12 48	
		596½	Crathes ... ... „	12 54	
		599	Banchory ... ... „	12 59	
Aberdeen		603⅜	Glassel ... ... „	1 10	
		606	Torphins ... ... „	1 15	
		609⅛	Lumphanan... ... „	1 23	
		611¾	Dess ... ... „	1 27	
		614½	Aboyne ... ... „	1 32	
		619	Dinnet ... ... „	1 41	
		621⅜	Cambus O'May ... „	1 46	
		625½	**Ballater** ... ...arr.	**1 55**	

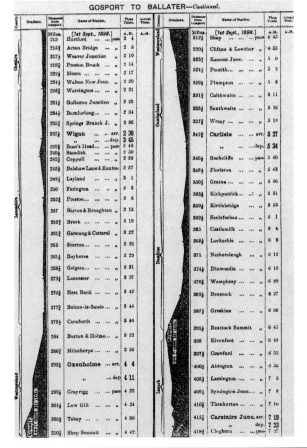

GOSPORT TO BALLATER—*Continued.*

County.	Gradient.	Distance from Gosport.	Name of Station.	Time Table.	Actual Time.
		Miles.	*[1st Sept., 1898.]*	A.M.	A.M.
Cheshire		213	Hartford ... ...pass	2 4	
		215¾	Acton Bridge ... „	2 8	
		217½	Weaver Junction „	2 10	
		219⅝	Preston Brook ... „	2 14	
		222½	Moore ... ... „	2 17	
		224½	Walton New Junc. „	2 20	
Lancashire		225⅝	Warrington ... ... „	2 21	
		231¼	Golborne Junction „	2 29	
		234½	Bamfurlong... ... „	2 34	
		235¾	Springs Branch J. „	2 36	
		237⅛	**Wigan** ... .. arr.	**2 38**	
			„ ... ...dep.	**2 45**	
		239⅜	Boar's Head... ... pass	2 48	
		240½	Standish ... ... „	2 50	
		242⅞	Coppull ... ... „	2 53	
		245⅜	Balshaw Lane & Euxton	2 57	
		248¼	Leyland ... ... „	3 1	
		250	Farington ... .. „	3 3	
		252⅝	Preston... ... ... „	3 8	
		257	Barton & Broughton „	3 15	
		259¾	Brock ... ... „	3 19	
		261¾	Garstang & Catteral „	3 22	
		265	Scorton... ... ... „	3 26	
		267½	Bayhorse ... ... „	3 29	
		268⅞	Galgate... ... ... „	3 31	
		273¼	Lancaster ... ... „	3 37	
		276⅜	Hest Bank ... ... „	3 42	
		277¾	Bolton-le-Sands ... „	3 44	
		279½	Carnforth ... ... „	3 46	
Westmoreland		284	Burton & Holme... „	3 52	
		286¾	Milnthorpe ... ... „	3 56	
		292¼	**Oxenholme** ... arr.	**4 4**	
			„ ... dep	**4 11**	
		299½	Grayrigg ... ... pass	4 22	
		301⅛	Low Gill ... ... „	4 24	
		305⅜	Tebay ... . „	4 30	
	SUMMIT	310⅞	Shap Summit ... „	4 42	

County.	Gradient.	Distance from Gosport.	Name of Station.	Time Table.	Actual Time.
		Miles.	*[1st Sept., 1898.]*	A.M.	A.M.
Westmoreland		312⅞	Shap ... ...pass	4 45	
		320¼	Clifton & Lowther „	4 55	
Cumberland		323⅜	Eamont Junc. ... „	5 0	
		324½	Penrith... ... ... „	5 2	
		329⅞	Plumpton ... ... „	5 8	
		331¾	Calthwaite ... ... „	5 11	
		335⅛	Southwaite ... ... „	5 16	
		337⅝	Wreay ... ... „	5 19	
		342⅜	**Carlisle** ... ... arr.	**5 27**	
			„ ... ...dep.	**5 34**	
		346½	Rockcliffe ... ...pass	5 40	
		348½	Floriston ... ... „	5 43	
Dumfries		350½	Gretna ... ... „	5 46	
		355⅞	Kirkpatrick... ... „	5 51	
		359⅛	Kirtlebridge ... „	5 56	
		362½	Ecclefechan ... ... „	6 1	
		365	Castlemilk ... ... „	6 4	
		368⅛	Lockerbie ... ... „	6 8	
		371	Nethercleugh ... „	6 12	
		374⅛	Dinwoodie ... ... „	6 16	
		376⅞	Wamphray ... ... „	6 20	
		382⅛	Beattock ... ... „	6 27	
		387⅜	Greskine ... ... „	6 36	
	SUMMIT	391⅛	Beattock Summit „	6 45	
Lanark		395	Elvanfoot ... ... „	6 49	
		397⅛	Crawford ... ... „	6 52	
		400¼	Abington ... ... „	6 56	
		405⅛	Lamington ... ... „	7 3	
		409¼	Symington Junc.... „	7 8	
		410⅞	Thankerton ... ... „	7 10	
		415⅞	**Carstairs Junc.** arr.	**7 18**	
			„ dep.	**7 23**	
		418⅝	Cleghorn ... ...pass	7 27	

Left Queen Victoria's timetable from Gosport to Ballater, Scotland (for Balmoral). It will be noted that the rail journey of 625½ miles took 18¼ hours, with just two refreshment stops en route, a quarter of an hour at Leamington and three-quarters of an hour at Perth! *By kind permission of Fareham Museum*

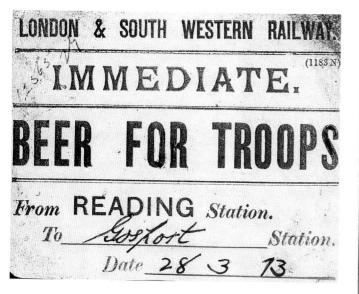

LONDON & SOUTH WESTERN RAILWAY.

IMMEDIATE.

(1183 N)

BEER FOR TROOPS

From READING Station.

To Gosport Station.

Date 28 3 13

Above A label dated 1913 attached to a very important consignment from Reading, Berkshire! *A. D. Davies collection*

Right Information to the general public regarding a special train in January 1959 to commemorate the centenary of the Direct Line from London to Gosport.

"THE PORTSMOUTH DIRECT LINE CENTENARIAN"

SUNDAY, 25th JANUARY 1959

To celebrate the Centenary of the opening to public traffic of the Godalming-Havant section of this line on 24th January 1859. (thus completing what subsequently became the principal rail artery from London to Portsmouth and the Isle of Wight arrangements have been made with Southern Region B.R. to run a SPECIAL COMMEMORATIVE TRAIN on the above date from Victoria (dep. 10.12 a.m.) to Gosport and back to Victoria (arr. 6.15 p.m. approx).

Outward Route. Victoria-Stewarts Lane-Pouparts Junction-Balham-Wimbledon-Oxshott-Clandon-Guildford-Godalming (Old Terminus)-Havant-Fareham-Gosport.

Return Route. As above to Guildford (omitting Godalming goods line), Woking-West Weybridge-Addlestone curve-Staines-Richmond, Clapham Junction-Ludgate Junction-Stewarts Lane-Victoria.

It will be noted that apart from the Godalming (terminus) and Fareham-Gosport lines and West Weybridge-Addlestone curve which are all "closed", other rarities such as Stewarts Lane-Pouparts Junction and the Surbiton-Effingham Junction section have been included. The latter is not known to have been traversed by a steam passenger train since the war.

Motive power. The train will be hauled by Adams Goods engine, 30567, from Victoria to Guildford and back. Only two of these engines, built in the 1880's now survive out of the original 70. As they appear to have no regular work, their early extinction is likely. This will almost certainly be your last chance to travel behind one of them. From Guildford to Gosport and back, motive power will be a Drummond 700 class Goods engine, which date from 1897.

Stock. One ex L. & S.W.R. coach will be included in the train, which will otherwise consist of B.R. open saloon coaches and "Hastings" type former Pullman Buffet Car.

Accommodation. For operating reasons, this will be severely limited and tickets sold will be limited to the train's seating capacity.

EARLY APPLICATION is, therefore, advised. It will definitely not be possible to strengthen the train in event of oversubscription.

Fare   26/6d adult from Victoria or Wimbledon.
        21/6d adult from Guildford or Godalming.
        20/- adult from Haslemere or Petersfield.

        Half fares will apply for accompanied juveniles under 14. Because of limited seating capacity, half fare tickets cannot be sold separately.

Intermediate stops. The train will call at Wimbledon at 10.39 a.m. Guildford 11.15 a.m. Godalming (goods) 1133 a.m. Haslemere 12.16 p.m. and Petersfield 12.34 p.m. to entrain passengers. On th return journey, it will call at Petersfield, Haslemere, Guildford and Clapham Junction only. There will also be service stops at Havant and Fareham in each direction.

To lend a topical and contemporary atmosphere to this event, it is expected that a party of people on the train will be attired in mid-Victorian costumes.

Applications for tickets and itinerary should be forwarded to G. R. Lockie, 36, Harold Road, London, S.E.19, enclosing remittance and s.a.e. They will be sent out about one week before 25th January 1959 but in event of oversubscription, you will be notified forthwith. Tickets from Guildford, Godalming, Haslemere and Petersfield may also be obtained from H. C. L. Grenside, "Wildlands" Corry Road, Hindhead Surrey.

Right One of the final rail tours run on the Gosport branch line was the RCTS 'Southdown Venturer' on 20 February 1966. Maunsell Class 'N' 2-6-0 No 31411 has just left Gosport station and is passing the site of the former engine shed (left). *Roger Bray collection*

Gosport railway station, pictured on a very murky day in December 1963. The line to Clarence Yard was situated between the platforms. This photograph was taken from the footbridge between the site of the engine shed and the signal box. *Bruce Oliver*

Left The railway triangle at Gosport, photographed on the same day. The left foreground is the rear of the site of the engine shed, which was still being used as a stabling point only a year previously. The Stokes Bay branch was reached via the left-hand side of the triangle, while straight ahead lies the route to Fareham. *Bruce Oliver*

Below left Gosport station in 1996, showing quite clearly how vegetation has taken over the trackbed and platforms. *Michael G. Harvey*

Below Another view of Gosport station building in 1996. Hampshire County Council has allocated £100,000 for renovating and tidying up the area. The railings and this 'Penfold' post-box have already been attended to. If an autumn 1996 £500,000 Lottery bid is successful, the site could be returned to public use with various uses; suggested include a railway museum, restaurant, craft workshops and a garden centre. *Eddie Rooke*

The Stokes Bay branch

The Stokes Bay & Isle of Wight Railway & Pier Company was formed in 1855 with a view to providing an easy link to the Isle of Wight from virtually its closest point on the mainland. The railway line was approximately 2 miles long from its junction just outside Gosport station to Stokes Bay pier, the departure point for the island steamers. The branch cost £24,000 to build, and opened on 6 April 1863; however, in its early days passengers were inconvenienced by the need to travel into Gosport station and back out again to Stokes Bay. Later the building of the triangle north of Gosport station removed this problem by allowing direct access to the pier via Stoke Road station (later Gosport Road).

In 1875 the LSWR took over the line and almost immediately provided a 2¾-hour Waterloo to Ryde service, half an hour quicker than could be achieved via Portsmouth. Unfortunately any increased traffic derived from this initiative was short-lived since Portsmouth Harbour station was opened the following year. This offered an alternative island route that did not suffer the sort of problems experienced at Stokes Bay pier, where the provision of services was often curtailed in bad weather. The steamer service was finally withdrawn in 1913.

The line continued to decline with the advent of trams, and was eventually closed to passengers on 1 November 1915, when, with the First World War in progress, the Admiralty requisitioned the pier and station. During the war the line was used to convey military goods, and in 1922 the Admiralty purchased the pier for £25,000 - only £1,000 more than the complete line had cost to build 59 years earlier! For a short while the line was used for stock storage, but by the late 1930s the railway track had been lifted.

Today a large part of the old route is a pleasant walk and cycle-way along which both the Workhouse and Little Anglesey viaducts still exist. However, apart from these the only remaining feature is a crossing-keeper's cottage at Stokes Bay (close to the start of the cycle-way), but it is also still possible to walk the complete route of the railway triangle on which the track was lifted in 1965.

Above A 1948 view of the trackbed of the former Stokes Bay branch and the Little Anglesey viaduct. To the right of the picture the now demolished bridge carrying Clayhall Road can be seen. *Denis Callender*

Right A December 1963 view of Stokes Bay pier shortly before its demolition. *Bruce Oliver*

The Lee-on-the-Solent branch

Having received parliamentary sanction in 1890, and after experiencing severe delays, the Lee-on-the-Solent Light Railway Company finally opened its line on 12 May 1894. It branched off the main line at Fort Brockhurst to reach its terminus just over 3 miles away, adjacent to the pier at Lee-on-the-Solent. The required land was obtained on a 99-year lease from the War Department, and although it owned its own carriages the company hired locomotives from the LSWR.

Apart from the two above-mentioned stations there were three request halts on the line at Privett (later renamed Fort Gomer Halt to avoid confusion with a similarly named station on the subsequently opened Meon Valley line), Browndown, and Elmore (the latter was not opened until 11 April 1910).

Although the line showed a deficit in its first year of operation, small profits were a regular feature in the early years until, in common with some of the other local seaside branch lines, competition from the buses reduced passenger levels. Notwithstanding this, and although having declined earlier opportunities to take over the line, the LSWR finally assumed control on 26 July 1909 and immediately introduced rail-motors, which, unlike those on the Southsea branch, could easily cope with the light demands of the line. In 1915 the operation was switched to push-pull workings utilising at first 'Terrier' tanks, then Class 'D1' 0-4-2 tanks.

During the First World War traffic actually increased on account of military construction work at Lee-on-the-Solent. In 1923 the Southern Railway reluctantly took over the line, and it was a little surprising that it continued to operate for a few more years before being closed to passengers on 31 December 1930, the halts having closed earlier in the year, on 1 May. Goods traffic continued for almost a further five years.

The bulk of the track had been lifted by 1940 and today, apart from the stations at Fort Brockhurst and Lee-on-the Solent (in use as a private residence and amusement arcade respectively), it is difficult to find any trace that the line ever existed.

The only readily apparent remnants of the former Lee-on-the-Solent branch are the former terminus station building at Lee-on-the-Solent (*left*), which is now in use as an amusement arcade, and Fort Brockhurst station, the only intermediate station between Fareham and Gosport and also the junction for the branch, which survives today as a private residence. As can be seen from this summer 1996 view (*below left*), the platforms are still intact. *Both Eddie Rooke*

The Bishops Waltham branch

Of all the closed lines covered in this chapter, quite probably the Bishops Waltham branch had the least chance of success since, apart from lacking, for example, the royal and military links and holiday trade of the other lines, this short branch was unfortunately never able to attract the necessary financial backing to expand; at various times connections to Droxford, Ropley, Winchester and Bursledon were planned.

The line opened on 1 June 1863 and ran for almost 4 miles from its junction with the main line at Botley to Bishops Waltham, closely following the course of the River Hamble virtually all the way. From the outset the Bishops Waltham Railway Company was beset with financial problems, partially caused by disappointing receipts, which resulted in its terminus station at Bishops Waltham not being finished until almost two years after the opening of the line. This station, replacing the temporary one used from the outset, was a most elaborate structure built by the local brickworks in a fashion that was no doubt meant to display the quality of their products.

With mounting financial pressures and the inability to attract capital investment for its expansion plans, in 1881 the company sold its whole undertaking to the LSWR for £22,000, although the latter company had for many years been working the line, retaining all the receipts and even incurring expenditure on capital items such as the two-road wooden engine shed at the terminus, built at a cost of £120 some four years earlier.

On the insistence of the Board of Trade, when the line opened it was worked by tank locomotives since the company was unable to finance a turntable at its terminus. Initial services comprised six trains in each direction, with three trains on Sundays. Rail-motors were introduced at the end of 1904 and ran for approximately ten years, but traffic continued to decline, especially during the First World War, forcing the Southern Railway to make economies early in 1931 by axing Sunday services (for the third time in the line's history) and closing the engine shed. But these measures were insufficient and the line closed to passengers on 31 December 1932, an event that attracted little attention in those days compared to similar events in more recent times. Freight workings, initially twice daily, continued, but these were soon reduced to daily and finally two or three times a week prior to final closure of the branch line on 27 April 1962.

Today a little of the old line remains in use - from the original bay platform at Botley station, Yeoman's aggregate trains, originating from Merehead, Somerset, work a short distance down the line to where an overhead conveying system empties the wagons and transfers the contents across the main lines and into bulk containers.

Apart from this, little now remains of the line. Nothing is left of Durley Halt (opened in 1910), while all the terminus buildings have been demolished. Only a set of level crossing gates at the start of a trackbed walk serves to remind of what was once a substantial station and goods yard, boasting an engine shed (formerly a sub-shed of Eastleigh), goods shed and water tower together with several private sidings serving the local brickworks, gas company and other outlets.

Shortly after the final closure an attempt was made by the Hampshire Narrow Gauge Railway Society to utilise part of the trackbed to lay a 2-foot gauge line, but this never came to fruition, in common with an earlier attempt by the same society to utilise part of the Meon Valley line. In 1996 this society's stock is dispersed around various sites, with one locomotive currently based on Hayling Island (of which more details will be given in the next chapter).

Just a short distance from where the Bishops Waltham branch joins the main line at Botley is 'Six Arches Viaduct', which nowadays can only be viewed in the winter months when the surrounding trees have shed their leaves. Pictured on the viaduct early in the century is an Adams 'Jubilee' 0-4-2 locomotive, many of which were at one time allocated to Fratton depot.
Gary Chase collection

Bishops Waltham station pictured in its last week before closure. The station canopy has been removed but the grand style of the buildings is readily apparent. *Bruce Oliver*

Enthusiasts' specials on the line were rare, with only three being recorded between 1952 and 1959. On 14 June 1952 tiny 'C14' Class 0-4-0 tank No 30589 hauls an RCTS special into Bishops Waltham station. *R. K. Blencowe collection*

Another view of Bishops Waltham station. Contrast the almost rural setting with what exists today! *Bruce Oliver*

Above An Ivatt Class '2MT' 2-6-2 tank locomotive shunts Bishops Waltham goods yard a few days before its closure; note the ornate goods shed. Another engine from this class, No 41328, worked the last train on the line. *Bruce Oliver*

In June 1863 *The Hampshire Telegraph* reported on the opening of the Bishops Waltham branch line with the following text:

The BISHOPS WALTHAM RAILWAY was opened for public traffic on MONDAY LAST; which made the little town full of bustle and life.

The beautiful toned bells of the old parish church were ringing a merry peal the whole of the day; and a celebrated brass band paraded the town. The BISHOPS WALTHAM Rifle Band also assisted. The principal gentlemen and tradesmen met at the CROWN HOTEL to inaugurate the opening of the railway. About 50 sat down to a dinner served up by MR. PRATT. MR A. HELPS ESQ, occupied the chair.

The SOUTH WESTERN RAILWAY COMP. was represented by MR. WHITNEY.

Above In the summer of 1996 all that remains at Bishops Waltham, apart from a trackbed walk, are these railway crossing gates situated on the town's busy roundabout, which obliterated the railway. Although the local authority is to be applauded for its information boards describing the line, it is a great pity that it was only able to find a picture of an Isle of Wight-liveried Class 'O2' 0-4-4 tank to illustrate the type of motive power once used on the line! *Eddie Rooke*

Right An August 1996 view of Botley station taken from the footbridge. The track of the Bishops Waltham line is still in place in the bay platform and the aggregate stone plant with its overhead conveyor can be seen in the background. *Eddie Rooke*

The Hayling Island branch

If you were to ask any railway enthusiast for the name of the closed railway line that he misses the most, the chances are that he would come up with the Somerset & Dorset, Great Central, Waverley, or some such similar main line. But ask anyone with an interest in railways in the South of England about the branch line that is most missed, it is almost certain that the Hayling line will be the most likely to be mentioned.

This excellent little holiday line, only 4½ miles in length, had a character of its own. It started from a bay platform at a busy main-line station, rapidly took you into beautiful countryside, across a large viaduct over the muddy waters of Langstone Harbour, and along an exposed coast line to the sandy beaches of your holiday destination, hauled by little Victorian vintage locomotives dwarfed by their coaching stock. Even in the 1960s this line, unlike many others up and down the country, was actually making a profit, but it had an 'Achilles' heel' in the form of its railway viaduct, which was, unfortunately, to bring about its downfall.

Hayling Island was first connected to the mainland in 1824 by means of a small bridge that was financed in the main by the Duke of Norfolk (the Lord of the Manor). In 1851 the Hayling Bridge & Causeway Company acquired this connection, having been authorised to build a horse-worked railway from Havant to Langstone, although this did not proceed at that time. However, once the LSWR reached Havant in 1859, plans for a Hayling Railway were resurrected with the Hayling Railway Company being formed by local businessmen in 1860. Additional Parliamentary authority was obtained in 1864 to build docks at Langstone and extend the proposed railway to South Hayling, and the first mile of track was opened from Havant to Langstone by mid-January 1865, for goods traffic only.

Following an abortive attempt to erect an embankment across the waters of Langstone Harbour to take the railway southwards to Sinah Point close to the Portsmouth Ferry landing stage (where large commercial docks were planned), work on the ultimate route commenced in 1867 under the guidance of the wealthy Francis Fuller, and the first train was able to run through to South Hayling on 28 June of that year. However, certain matters relating to the track needed to be rectified to meet the requirements of the Board of Trade Inspector before the line could be opened on 17 July to coincide with the second day of the Hayling Races on Sinah Common.

There were four stations on the line, Havant, Langstone, North Hayling and Hayling Island.

Havant This was the connection to the main line where the Hayling train had the sole use of a bay platform and watering and coaling facilities.

Langstone The LBSCR dropped the 'E' from Langstone soon after taking control of the line. This halt had a small single platform, together with a signal box, waiting room/ticket office and level crossing, which, at busy times, especially summer weekends and holidays, was the cause of substantial traffic jams; in fact, at those times two men were needed to shut the gates against the heavy volume of traffic.

North Hayling This second halt on the line was situated in a very exposed coastal position and comprised only a wooden platform and a very basic waiting room. A small siding was built, used more in the early days for the oyster trade in the harbour.

Hayling Island This was known as South Hayling in its early years and was situated half a mile from the beach. The station was quite a substantial affair comprising a sizeable building that included facilities for passengers, two platforms, sidings and a goods shed, together with coaling and watering facilities for the locomotives.

With a virtually flat landscape to run across, the line had very few notable sights en route except of course for the viaduct across Langstone Harbour. This was an impressive structure with 1,100 feet of wooden trestles incorporating a central swing bridge to allow small boats, etc, to pass to and fro between Langstone and Chichester Harbours. Until just before the start of the Second World War a small signal box situated on the bridge was manned by a signalman to open and close the bridge.

At the northern end of the viaduct it is still possible to discern today where a train ferry terminal previously existed. For almost three years, between 1885 and 1888, a paddle-steamer named *Carrier* operated a regular railway wagon service to St Helens on the Isle of Wight, but the silting up of Langstone Harbour contributed to the short-lived nature of this exercise.

When the line first opened, six return trips were provided on weekdays (soon reduced to four), but in the holiday boom years of the early 1960s the summer Saturday timetable showed no fewer than 24 trains per day - even on Sundays 21 trains were scheduled with journey times between 10 and 13 minutes, depending on whether or not the trains stopped at the halts on the line. In the latter years of the line most trains comprised between one and three coaches with the then modern-day coaching stock dwarfing the diminutive locomotives. Freight trains, as such, did not run. Instead, goods vehicles were incorporated into certain timetabled passenger services.

The line was worked by the contractor's locomotives from the outset until the end of 1871, when the line was leased to the LBSCR at £2,000 per annum (it was subsequently absorbed by the Southern Railway in 1923). A variety of small engines was initially used, limited of course by the weight restrictions on the bridge over the harbour. Between 1874 and 1889 two Sharp Stewart 2-4-0 tank engines named, rather appropriately, *Hayling Island* and *Fratton* were employed on the line. Following their departure Stroudley's 'Terrier' locomotives made their first appearances, commencing what was to be a permanent occupation of the line right up to its closure in 1963. From time to time consideration was given to replacement locomotives, but trials with a 'P' Class tank in 1957 came to nothing, as did plans to upgrade the line to use the larger 'M7s'.

When the line was first opened its locomotives were initially serviced in a small engine shed situated south of the former A27 road into Havant. In 1874 this facility was replaced by another single-road engine shed (previously erected at Petworth), which was installed at South Hayling before being demolished in 1894 when all the servicing of the line's locomotives was carried out at Fratton depot.

Unfortunately, although the line appeared to remain profitable, the decaying state of the viaduct would apparently have necessitated replacement at a cost of approximately £400,000, and closure notices were posted at the end of 1962, resulting in the last timetabled service being run on 2 November 1963, followed by the Locomotive Club of Great Britain's 'Hayling Farewell' rail tour, run on the next day.

Although attempts were made locally to re-open the line, these did not come to fruition owing to factors such as finance, the state of the viaduct and the need for the proposed Havant bypass to cross the trackbed south of Havant town centre. One scheme put forward was to electrify the line with overhead wires and use electric tram cars - indeed, a 1939-built Blackpool tram arrived in September 1965 and resided in Havant goods yard until the scheme collapsed, when it was transferred to an East Anglian Transport Museum in 1969. The dismantling of the track commenced in January 1967.

Today there is little evidence that this line existed - the bay platform and siding at Havant are now a car park, the rest of the line has become the Hayling Billy Coastal Path Walk. Some of the few items that still remain can be seen in the accompanying photographs. One other interesting remnant is the canopy from Hayling station, which was saved and installed at the Hollycombe Steam Collection near Liphook, Hampshire.

The viaduct, however, refuses to die. In July 1996 Havant Borough Council were considering a £1.5m project to re-instate the bridge to cater solely for pedestrians and cyclists who are in danger using the present road bridge, which carries approximately 20,000 vehicles per day. The proposed bridge would either be tall enough for boats to pass underneath or a swing bridge would once again be incorporated.

A member of the station staff is about to accept the single-line 'token' from the driver of Class 'A1X' 0-6-0T No 32670 as it steams into Hayling Island station on a Saturday in July 1961. The next train to Havant awaits departure from the adjoining platform. No 32670 lives on today in the company of No 32650 on the Kent & East Sussex Railway. *Bruce Oliver*

Left Havant station in the late 1950s - Class 'A1X' 0-6-0T No 32661 rests between its duties on the Hayling Island branch, with Driver Bill Anderson (left) and his fireman posed alongside. The wagons in the up sidings (extreme left) are wooden hoppers as used in permanent way trains - the wording reads 'EMPTY TO HAVANT'. Also of interest is the station sign (extreme right), which reads 'HAVANT FOR HAYLING ISLAND'. No 32661 was, unfortunately, one of the few latter-day 'Terriers' not to pass into preservation, being scrapped in 1963. *Pat Anderson collection*

Below left Class 'A1X' No 32640 has just arrived at Havant station with its train from Hayling Island in the early 1960s. This particular engine had the distinction of being the first 'Terrier' to steam into Portsmouth when it arrived to be transported by ship to Dieppe for display at the Paris International Exhibition in 1878. Over a century later No 32640 survives on the Isle of Wight Steam Railway - but the platform and sidings area depicted here have now been converted to a car park. *Bruce Oliver*

Top On 26 October 1963, a week before the closure of the Hayling branch line, Class 'A1X' No 32650 emerges from beneath the road bridge that used to carry the A27 traffic prior to the bypass being built. Apart from a footbridge just south of this location, this was the only over-bridge on the line. Today part of the trackbed only a few yards away serves as a car park for the nearby Havant Museum, which continually resurrects memories of the line with its model railway displays and photographs. No 32650 went to the Kent & East Sussex Railway after withdrawal from BR. *Bruce Oliver*

Middle 'Terrier' No 32662 enters Langstone station on 21 July 1963. The only easily recognisable trace of the railway remaining today at this location is the cottage to the right of the engine. No 32662 survives at the Bressingham Steam Museum, Norfolk, after a period of 'static display' at a Butlin's Holiday Camp. *Bruce Oliver*

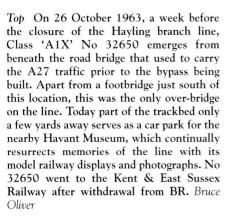

Bottom A driver's-eye view of the Langstone viaduct. Note the spark-arrestor fitted to the chimney of the 'A1X', essential in view of the wooden structure of the viaduct. *Eric Grace*

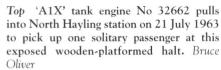

Top 'A1X' tank engine No 32662 pulls into North Hayling station on 21 July 1963 to pick up one solitary passenger at this exposed wooden-platformed halt. *Bruce Oliver*

Middle On the last day of timetabled trains, 2 November 1963, Class 'A1X' No 32662 enters Hayling Island station. Note the wreath on the smokebox door, which the engine carried for most of the day. *Bruce Oliver*

Bottom On 26 October 1963 the fireman shovels coal into 'Terrier' No 32650's bunker from the basic coaling stage at Hayling Island terminus. The goods shed in the background was the only structure that avoided demolition after the closure of the line. *Bruce Oliver*

Above right On the Sunday following closure, 3rd November 1963, the Locomotive Club of Great Britain ran a 'Hayling Farewell' rail tour (which also visited Portsmouth Royal Naval Dockyard). Following a trip up and down the Hayling branch behind Class 'A1X' 0-6-0 tanks Nos 32636 and 32670, the rail tour is seen preparing to leave Havant for its return to London (Victoria) hauled by Maunsell Class 'Q' 0-6-0s Nos 30531 and 30543. *Bruce Oliver*

Right Pictured in Havant station goods yard is the former Blackpool tram, which, it was hoped, would provide the necessary impetus to re-open the Hayling Island branch line using overhead electrification. *Bruce Oliver*

My six years on the railway

by Dave Pallett

I started work on the railway at Fratton in 1959, after first being sent to Eastleigh for a medical and eyesight test. I began work as a roster clerk's assistant, which involved being tea boy and other duties such as being sent out to a local driver's or fireman's home to 'knock them up' whenever a change of turn was needed urgently!

After a few months I was sent to Guildford to be taught the art of looking after a steam locomotive's boiler; I also had an insight into the BR Rule Book and, following a seven-day course, I was passed as a cleaner. My first taste of the shovel was to assist 'Jumbo' Collis, who was the crane man in charge of DS 200 at the small coal stage in Fratton depot yard.

As a passed cleaner I was often sent 'on loan' to help out at other engine sheds such as Guildford and Nine Elms. Having at a later date (1962) learned the skills of firing a BR steam locomotive, I had my first main-line experience of a footplate turn while 'on loan' to Nine Elms. In fact, my duty for that day merely involved preparing an engine and taking it 'light' to Waterloo and preparing it ready for a main-line turn, then transferring to the incoming passenger train and returning 'light' to Nine Elms. But due to the much delayed up train the driver and I were told to work a 'Merchant Navy' Class 'Pacific' on an express train bound for Bournemouth!

By the time we were relieved at Southampton Central station by an Eastleigh crew, I could still feel the after-effects of the heat and sweat, and as I sat in the comfort of one of the recently introduced 'Hampshire' diesel units, which took me home via Netley to Portsmouth, I realised that I had just had a very memorable experience on the footplate of a main-line locomotive, as I would not normally be firing at this level.

My duties also took me over to the Isle of Wight to work the lines from Ryde to Cowes and Ventnor. On the latter run, if you were having a 'rough 'un' with one of the Class 'O2' 0-4-4 tanks, the driver would not depart from Wroxall unless sufficient steam and water was in the boiler - he did not want to run the risk of having to stop in the tunnel under St Boniface Down. While steam was being raised he used the cafe on the up platform to fill up the tea can!

My turns from Fratton depot included such locations as Salisbury, Basingstoke, Eastleigh, Guildford, Littlehampton, Gosport and the Hayling Island branch. On the Hayling Island weekday service the early shift crew prepared the 'Terrier' 'A1X' Class tank engines and on Monday mornings took the empty carriages to Havant; later in the morning they would clean the clinker from the fire. The late shift crew would travel on an ordinary service train to Havant and work the afternoon shift, then bring the empty carriages back to Fratton sidings on Sunday night for cleaning and servicing. Just after midday a cleaner would be sent from Fratton depot to Hayling to coal up the engine. This was done from a small coaling stage, and at the same time he would shovel up all the clinker and ash from the engine's firebox and put it into an empty wagon. Often my brother Rick (a cleaner at this date) would help me with this job. Then, with the driver's permission, I would drive and Rick would fire on the train to Havant. I recall that we had a regular footplate passenger (unofficial) - a certain Mr Alan Bell would be present with his camera, and I think he must have photographed just about every nut and bolt on the Hayling Island branch!

On a summer weekend three 'Terriers' would be used and the bay platform at Hayling Island station would come into use. The last up train of the day would stop at North Hayling Halt to pick up the single platform lamp, and sometimes we even picked up a passenger or two!

For a driver and fireman on the Hayling line, the winter months and during bad weather conditions proved to be one of the most difficult of turns - it certainly was not one that we looked forward to. We had to endure the prevailing south-westerly winds and gales while on the viaduct, and the crew were wide open to the elements! To help get some protection from the wind and rain we would tie a tarpaulin over one side of the engine cab.

I had the pleasure of working with a variety of different drivers and firemen. My final regular driver was George 'Jock' MacAskill, and together we worked the final train out from Hayling Island in 1963 on the footplate of 'A1X' No 32670; another 'A1X' was at the rear of this train with driver Ray Forder and fireman Micky Lee in charge.

I recall that the signalman at Langstone crossing gates had a novel sideline in that he hand-made plastic windmills! He would display his wares on a mound of earth beside the level crossing for all to see, and as a result he would inevitably sell them to children - this he did while the traffic waited for the train to pass. He would especially attract the attention of children who were en route to the seaside with their parents.

My memories include some amusing events, including the night that detonators were put in the sand-drying furnace when a couple of platelayers had dozed off to sleep on the dry sand - they went off with quite a bang, and watching the startled men run off was quite an amusing experience! I once had an extremely damp experience, in that I had a shunter's pole stuck through the arms of my overalls and was held up underneath a fully turned on water column, the only consolation being that it was a hot summer's day!

One of the engine duties of the night shift at Fratton depot was to 'fill the boiler to the whistle' (in simple terms this meant filling the boiler right up and reducing

It is 10.25 pm on 2 November 1963, and the last train of the day from Hayling Island has just arrived at Havant station. The engine is Class 'A1X' 0-6-0 tank No 32662, and coupled to her, out of sight, is fellow 'A1X' No 32650. Although this was an ordinary service train, note the wreath displayed on the coal bunker to commemorate the final week of trains on the Hayling Island branch. In the cab is driver George 'Jock' MacAskill, standing on the footplate is fireman Dave Pallett, and on the platform is porter Albert Grout (in raincoat) and John Cherrison, porter/ticket collector. *By kind permission of Alan A. F. Bell*

the pressure), then 'black' the firebox with layers of coal dust. When this had been completed it was a quick walk down Goldsmith Avenue to the Railway Rifle Social Club for a welcome pint of ale. If in the meantime someone moved that engine it would quickly pick up its water and plumes of watery black smoke would come drifting out of its chimney, giving it the appearance of a 'wet volcano'!

In the latter years of my job on BR I can recall working the 9.30 am Portsmouth to Cardiff passenger as far as Salisbury. On this particular turn we had Standard Class '4' 2-6-0 No 76069, which was in a run-down condition and leaked steam from all angles. To help gain some time and to get the boiler pressure up, we unofficially took on water at Southampton Central station. We then made it as far as Dean, where we stopped for a 'blow-up' as we were short of steam - after building up enough pressure we continued to Salisbury and our arrival time was considerably later than scheduled. On arrival at Salisbury shed my driver, 'Jock' MacAskill, demanded a change of locomotive for the return journey to Portsmouth!

I left the railway in April 1964. My six years employed by BR had been thoroughly satisfying, and I was being paid for a job that I enjoyed doing. Today I am still involved with steam trains, albeit as a volunteer on the Mid-Hants Railway (the Watercress Line), driving and firing the type of locomotives that I was accustomed to in my BR days.

Class 'A1X' 0-6-0 tank engine No 32646 crosses Langstone viaduct with a down train on 29 July 1963. At this date the 'Terriers' were allocated to Eastleigh depot and the white numberplate, buffers and smokebox door brackets were the work of that shed's staff - but for what reason remains a mystery. *Bruce Oliver*

No 32646 - this is your life!

Built at Brighton Works in 1876 as one of a class of 50 engines designed by William Stroudley to work primarily in the London area, No 46 *Newington* (its original number) has spent the bulk of its 120 years in close proximity to Portsmouth.

It commenced its working life in January 1877 in the London area, but in 1903, having clocked up over half a million miles and having been renumbered 646, it was sold for £500 to the LSWR for use on its newly constructed Lyme Regis branch. There it was renumbered yet again to LSWR No 734, but within two years the increas-

ing traffic, especially at holiday times, was preventing it from performing totally effectively, and from 1906 it could therefore be found operating in such diverse places as Yeovil, Bournemouth, Exmouth Junction and the Bishops Waltham branch.

It was loaned to the Freshwater, Yarmouth & Newport Railway on the Isle of Wight in 1913 prior to a sale in 1914 at a price of £900, when it was renumbered once more to FY&NR No 2. Ten years later, having been absorbed by the Southern Railway, it was renumbered W2 and in 1928 was renamed *Freshwater*, before being renumbered yet again to W8. It remained on the Isle of Wight until 1949, when it returned to the mainland, via Southampton Docks, and spent many years working the Hayling Island branch, renumbered as BR No 32646.

Following the closure of the Hayling line it was towed from Fratton depot to Eastleigh by classmate No 32662 on 2 January 1964, after which it ran under its own steam in November 1964 from Eastleigh to its new base at Droxford station on the disused Meon Valley line, having been sold to the Sadler Railcar Company.

In 1966 it was purchased by the Portsmouth-based brewery Brickwoods, who steamed it for a final run to Knowle and back on 13 May 1966, before transferring it a few days later to the Hayling Billy public house on Hayling Island, where it was to remain as a static exhibit until June 1979, when it returned to the Isle of Wight. It was overhauled and returned to working service in 1981, but in the summer of 1996 it was awaiting further major repairs and is the subject of an appeal.

Following withdrawal from BR and a spell at Droxford on the Meon Valley line, No 32646 was restored to her original LBSCR 'Stroudley green' livery and displayed between 1966 and 1979 as No 46 *Newington* as a 'static exhibit' in the car park at the Hayling Billy public house on Hayling island. *Bruce Oliver*

June 1996 found No 32646 in the guise of No W8 *Freshwater* exhibited at Haven Street on the Isle of Wight Steam Railway pending major overhaul. *Eddie Rooke*

Above The remains of the Langstone railway viaduct in the summer of 1996, looking towards Havant.
Will it be rebuilt in due course for the use of pedestrians and cyclists? *Eddie Rooke*

Below The former goods shed at Hayling Island station has now been incorporated into a new Arts Theatre Development, which was opened in 1996. *Eddie Rooke*

Below right Somehow this signal post, situated just south of the viaduct, has survived to 1996 and has not been removed for further use on one of today's preserved railways. *Eddie Rooke*

The Southsea Railway

This very small line, just 1¼ miles long, had the shortest life of any standard gauge railway covered in this book. It opened on 1 July 1885 and closed just over 29 years later on the outbreak of war in 1914.

Its existence really came about because of the need for Victorian holidaymakers to get to the seaside and steamers to the Isle of Wight, and one particular man's strong ambitions to build the line. It is worth noting that Fratton station might never have been created had it not been for this line, and instead Copnor might have had the station its inhabitants were always clamouring for.

The idea of a line to the seaside had been considered (and discounted) by the LBSCR and LSWR soon after their respective railways arrived in Portsmouth, since they realised that, with the existing line needing to terminate at Portsmouth station, as the military authorities were unwilling to let them breach the town's fortifications, they were unable to run direct to the edge of Portsmouth Harbour - an ideal starting point for travellers to the Isle of Wight. The situation was further

aggravated when the line to Stokes Bay Pier opened in 1863, giving easy access to the Isle of Wight.

In 1861 Southsea Pier (later renamed Clarence Pier) had opened and steamers to the Isle of Wight called there. Unfortunately rail travellers arriving at Portsmouth had a journey of about a mile to get there, and a cab was necessary until 1865 when the Landport & Southsea Tramway Company opened a horse-drawn service from the station to the pier.

The following year (1866) the idea of a railway to the more heavily populated areas of Southsea was resurrected by a consortium including a certain Edwin Galt, who was in due course to become the Mayor of Portsmouth. In August 1867 Parliament approved a scheme that would have seen the new line branching off the existing main line just south of St Mary's Road Bridge (and just north of the then non-existent Fratton station) and also connecting the proposed Southsea station to Portsmouth station by a direct line through Fratton. However, two years later the scheme was abandoned on account of lack of financial backing, with neither of the local railway companies interested in participating.

Almost ten years elapsed before there was major activity again on the Southsea Railway front, and in the meantime, in 1876, the station at Portsmouth Harbour was opened and the tramway to Clarence Pier lost a vast amount of its traffic with rail travellers naturally preferring the ease of connecting with the Isle of Wight steamers at the new station. At about this time a new pier, South Parade Pier, was opened.

In late 1878 new plans for a Southsea Railway were laid, and the railway companies agreed to provide a station at Fratton subject to certain conditions. However, in the same month Galt and his colleagues deposited plans for a new station at Copnor with a new line running parallel to the main line. However, following pressure from the railway companies the plans were changed yet again to a simple connection at Fratton. The appropriate act for the new line was passed in August 1880, but Galt's enterprise was once again unable to attract sufficient financial backing, and he surprisingly turned down a substantial joint offer by the railway companies. Nevertheless, by the end of 1882 he had managed to persuade the LSWR to go behind the LBSCR's back and put up the bulk of the monies in an amended scheme that did not connect with Portsmouth station. Construction work finally started in early 1884, and the double-track railway, with an elaborate three-platform terminus at Granada Road, Southsea, opened on 1 July 1885.

Within a year the line was sold, in equal shares, to the joint committee of the LSWR and LBSCR, who agreed to operate the line in alternate years. Although the railway seemed to pay its way for its first decade, increasing

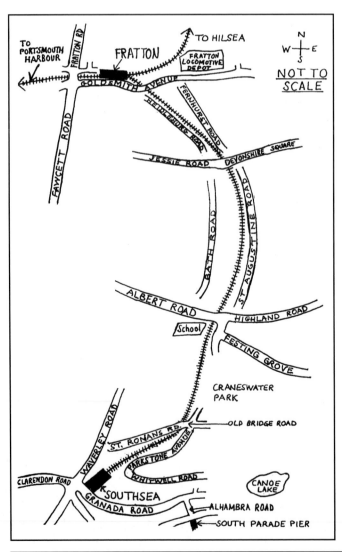

The route of the Southsea Railway showing the approximate locations of roads in close proximity to the line. *Michael G. Harvey*

competition from the trams started to have an effect and the railway went into decline, accentuated in 1901 when the tramways began to be converted to electric power. In 1903, to counter this, the joint committee decided upon a series of radical measures, which included using only one track, new halts at Jessie Road and Albert Road (opened in 1904), a move to a new, smaller station in close proximity to the old one, and a substantial reduction in personnel and motive power costs by the introduction of two steam rail-motors. Unfortunately these proved to be under-powered, with 'banking' by steam locomotives commonplace; rebuilding with new boilers was necessary almost from the outset.

These measures arrested the financial decline initially, but by 1912 losses were again increasing substantially. Nevertheless, the joint committee (by then working the line in five-year cycles) did not seem to have the inclination to close the branch since extensive repairs were carried out on the rail-motors around this time. However, following the outbreak of the First World War the following notice was displayed at Fratton: 'NO MOOR TRANES TO EAST SOUTHSEA, FISHAL.'

The final train ran on 8 August 1914. During the war years the line was used for military storage, and although it was expected to re-open when hostilities ceased, confirmation of its closure was announced in 1919.

The whole of the line was virtually level throughout its 1¼ miles, with no major constructions apart from four bridges (at Goldsmith Avenue, Jessie Road, Albert Road and St Ronans Road). Today no trace remains of any of these or the two

The Southsea Railway did not receive a good press, as this extract from the *Evening News* of 2 July 1885 shows:

Who does the Southsea Railway benefit, and who are the people it inconveniences? So far as we are able to ascertain, it benefits nobody, except the owners of the waste and hitherto profitless land at the eastern end of Southsea, who hope that shops will now arise where formerly thistles and shingle have exercised a disputed ownership. It inconveniences thousands of people who every day throng in and out of the Portsmouth Station, whose trains not only have an additional stopping place, but are brought into the Portsmouth Town Station at a much slower rate than was formerly the case.

By kind permission of THE NEWS *(formerly the* Evening News) *Portsmouth*

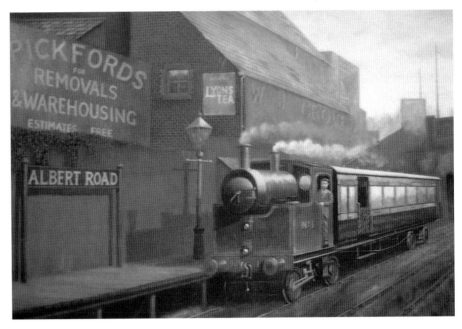

Above right In an effort to achieve financial stability on the branch two steam rail-motors were introduced in 1903. No 1 is shown at Albert Road Halt, which was opened in July 1904 with Jessie Road Halt, in an attempt to attract more passengers. After withdrawal the boiler of this rail-motor was eventually to find further local use at Fratton locomotive depot on the engineer's crane. *From an original painting by Graham Beech, by courtesy of John Harris; photograph by Bruce Oliver*

Right 'Terrier' 0-6-0T No 48 *Leadenhall* is depicted waiting to depart for Southsea from the branch platform at Fratton. Built in late 1876, this engine arrived in Portsmouth in 1890 and, apart from working to East Southsea, was one of the first 'Terriers' to work the Hayling Island branch. It was scrapped in 1901. *From an original painting by Graham Beech, by courtesy of John Harris; photograph by Bruce Oliver*

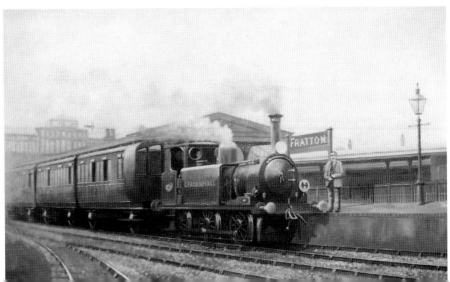

halts. Until very recently parts of the terminus at Southsea still existed (in use within a large garage and car sales area), but these have now been obliterated by a housing development. With prior knowledge of the railway's route it is still possible to recognise the path of the line along the curving contours of certain roads - but little else remains to remind one of the railway's existence.

Unfortunately the Southsea Railway did not seem to have attracted photographers, with only a handful of views in existence. Hopefully the accompanying reproductions of oil paintings by local artist Graham Beech (and that on the back cover) will give the reader an idea of the motive power used on the line.

The Meon Valley line

The Meon Valley line differed from the other closed lines described in this chapter in that it did not have a terminus at one end - instead it had busy junctions at each end in the form of Fareham and Alton. However, this did not enable it to attract sufficient traffic levels, and even though it was constructed to main-line standards, its life span was only just over 50 years.

Almost a century after its opening the reasons for its construction by the LSWR are not totally clear. A common line of thought is that it was built for military reasons, since it offered an alternative connection from Aldershot to the South Coast, but there has never been any concrete evidence to support this. More likely is the

opinion that it was constructed for defensive reasons to prevent the Great Western Railway from getting a foothold in the area (the GWR had already reached Basingstoke, Winchester and Southampton), and additionally to counter the threat of the proposed construction of the Portsmouth, Basingstoke & Godalming Railway, which had strong backing from the people of Portsmouth. As an alternative the LSWR undertook to construct a 'Light Railway' between Basingstoke and Fareham, but ultimately decided to build the section between Alton and Fareham to main-line standards; however, although the necessary land was acquired and the line's two large tunnels and bridges were constructed to take double tracks, only a single track was ever laid.

Although late arriving on the scene, in 1903, there had been diverse schemes for railways in the valley for over 50 years, with connections planned at various times at such locations as Petersfield, Ropley and Farnham. Approval for the eventual scheme of 22½ miles was obtained in June 1897. Construction commenced in 1898, with an estimated cost of £348,214 (had the 'Light Railway' been built the cost would have been approximately £150,000) - the final cost was £377,709. The contractors, apart from having trouble attracting sufficient labour, experienced several major problems with both clay and chalk cuttings, construction of the two tunnels (West Meon, 539 yards, and Privett, 1,056 yards), and the erection of the viaduct at West Meon, which was originally planned to be of concrete construction.

Auto-trains formed the bulk of the passenger traffic on the Meon Valley line for most of its history. This one, propelled by a Class 'M7'

0-4-4 tank, even has a goods van attached to the front of the engine. The train is seen arriving at Fareham station. *Denis Callender*

A 'King Arthur' Class 4-6-0 locomotive passes through Knowle Halt towards Fareham with a mixed freight in the late 1950s. This halt, situated close to the junction of the Meon Valley and Fareham to Eastleigh lines, opened on 1 May 1907 and was originally known as Knowle Asylum Halt, since it served the local mental hospital; visiting day was Thursday, so many trains only stopped there on that day. The sidings here closed in 1962, with the station closing on 6 April 1964 followed by the signal box on 6 May 1973 when the route to Botley was reduced to a single line. *Lens of Sutton*

Accordingly the official opening of the line was almost a year behind schedule. and when this took place on 1 June 1903 it was a very low-key affair; apart from garden parties for the upper class, the only item of note was the offer of free single journeys to the next station, the only drawback being the need to purchase a ticket to return to one's starting point or suffer a long walk!

Each of the line's five stations possessed extensive buildings (incorporating accommodation for the respective station masters), goods sidings and 600-foot platforms to main-line standard to accommodate ten-coach trains, which, apart from enthusiasts' specials in its final year, never materialised. Additional goods sidings were provided at Mislingford and Farringdon (which later acquired halt status in 1931).

In the early days of the line some Waterloo to Gosport services were diverted over this new route, but the potential of this was never fully realised, and the arrival of the third rail electrification to Alton in 1937 reduced the number of through trains from Waterloo, since they now, in the main, terminated at Alton. The bulk of passenger services were therefore local ones between Alton, Fareham and Gosport, but considering the rural nature of the line, one could never really have expected the line to be profitable. Indeed, freight traffic, in particular milk, timber, coal, livestock and fruit, was perhaps the main reason the whole line managed to survive until 1955, when the section between Farringdon and Droxford was closed, allowing freight to continue a little longer on the two remaining sections - Knowle to Droxford lasted until 30 April 1962, while the Farringdon service survived until 13 August 1968.

Passenger services had previously been withdrawn on Saturday 5 February 1955, with Class 'M7' tank No 30055 and Class '700' 0-6-0 No 30326 working the last trains. The following day an enthusiasts' special, headed by a pair of 'T9' 4-4-0s, Nos 30301 and 30732, having first visited the Midhurst branch, which had also formally closed on the previous day, made a final run up the Meon Valley line to Alton and onwards to Waterloo.

Today a large part of this previously picturesque line has returned to nature - cuttings have been filled in, the West Meon viaduct removed, the stations at Wickham and West Meon demolished. However, three of the stations have been converted to homes, and the line can still be traversed in part on foot along the trackbed between West Meon and Wickham.

MEON VALLEY (ALTON AND FAREHAM) LINE.

FOR SPEED RESTRICTIONS SEE PAGES A, B, C, D, E, F & G.

This is a Single Line from Butts Junction to Fareham Junction and is worked under the Regulations for working Single Lines by the Electric Train Tablet Block System.

UP TRAINS.—WEEK DAYS. / SUNDAYS

Distance from Gosport.	Nos.	1 Pass.		2 Pass.		3 Pass. Eastleigh. B		4 Special Discharged Soldiers when req'd.		5 Pass. F		6 Pass.		7 Goods. D		8 Pass.		9 Pass.		1 Pass. Portsmouth.		2 Pass. Portsmouth.	
M. C.		arr.	dep.	arr.	dep.	arr.	dep.	arr.	dep.	arr.	dep.	arr.	dep.	arr.	dep.	arr.	dep.	arr.	dep.	arr.	dep.	arr.	dep.
		a.m.	a.m.	a.m.	a.m.	a.m.	a.m.	a.m.	a.m.	p.m.	p.m.	p.m.	p.m.	p.m.	p.m.	p.m.	p.m.	p.m.	p.m.	a.m.	a.m.	p.m.	p.m.
— —	Gosport	...	725	...	...	...	...	...	...	...	...	...	...	...	...	...	5 5	...	...	...	...	...	...
1 36	Fort Brockhurst	7 28	7 29	...	...	...	...	...	11 38	...	...	...	...	...	...	5 8	5 9	...	...	...	...	...	...
5 0	Fareham	735	740	...	1039	...	1130	11 15		...	1 37	...	430	...	5 5	515	526	...	6 47	826	830	726	728
7 6	Knowle Platf'rm			Aft. No.1 Dn	10 44	Aft. No 1 Dn	11 34	Aft.No.4 Dn		Aft.No.6 Dn		Aft.No.6 Dn		Aft.No6Dn		Aft. No.7 Dn						Aft. 1 Du.	
7 31	Knowle Box	7 45		10 45		11 39		11 50		1 42		4 35		5 13 D		5 31		6 51 6 52		8 35		7 33	
9 13	Wickham	7 48	7 49	10 48	1049	11B42	...	11 53		1 45	1 46	4 38	4 39	5 18	5 46	5 34	5 35	6 53 6 56	6 57	8 38 8 39		7 36 7 37	
				Cross No.2 Down.				Cross Nos. 2 & 3 Down.						Fol.No. 8 Up		Precede No. 7 Up							
11 8	Mislingford Gds.	...	...	...	...	...	...	...	...	...	...	...	...	5 51	6 5	...	...	...	...	...	...	...	...
16 23	Droxford	7 58	7 59	10 58	10 59	...	...	12 2		1 55	1 56	4 48	4 49	6 14	6 35	5 44	5 45	7 6	7 7	8 48 8 49		7 46 7 47	
														Cross No. 7 Down.									
18 11	West Meon	8 6	8 7	7 11	6 11 7	...	...	12 9		2 3	2 4	4 56	4 58	6 45	7 34	5 52	5 53	7 14	7 15	8 56 8 57		7 54 7 55	
														Cross No.8 Dwn. & Fol. No. 9 Up.									
22 19	Privett	8 16	8 17	11 16	11 17	...	...	12 18		2 13	2 14	5 7	5 8	7 46	8 2	6 2	6 5	7 24	7 25	9 6	9 7	8 4 8 5	
25 32	Tisted	8 22	8 23	11 22	11 23	...	...	Crs.No.4 Dn. 12 22		2 19	2 20	5 13	5 14	8 10	8 20	Crs.No.7Dn 6 10	6 11	Crs.No.8 Dn 7 30	7 31	9 12 9 13		8 10 8 11	
27 12	Faringdon Gds.	...	...	Crs.No 3 Du.		...	...	...	...	...	...	...	...	8 25	8 35	...	...	...	...	...	...	...	...
29 53	Butts Junction	8 29		11 29		...	...	12 27		...	2 26	...	5 20		8 40	...	...	...	...	9 19		8 17	
30 61	Alton	8 31	8 48	11 31	1136	...	...	12 39		2 28	2 31	522	532	8 45	...	6 19	657	7 39	7 58	9 21 9 24		8 19 8 25	
77 56	Waterloo	1021	...	1 0		...	...	2 3		4 13		7 1		...	...	846	...	9 29		1148		10 9	

DOWN TRAINS.—WEEK-DAYS. / SUNDAYS.

Distance from Waterloo	Nos.	1 Pass.		2 Goods. A		3 Pass.		4 Pass. E		5 Pass. Eastleigh. C		6 Pass. G		7 Pass.		8 Pass.		1 Pass Portsm'th		2 Pass Portsm'th	
M. C.		arr.	dep.	arr.	dep.	arr.	dep.	arr.	dep.	arr.	dep.	arr.	dep.	arr.	dep.	arr.	dep.	arr.	dep.	arr.	dep.
— —	Waterloo	..	7 10	...	...	...	9 20	...	9 50	...	...	...	1 10	...	4 12	...	5 30	...	8 50	...	6 10
46 75	Alton	8 46	8 58	...	9 6	1059	1110	1149	noon 12 0	...	...	3 2	3 9	5 42	5 46	6 57	7 4	1044	1050	...	8 20
46 3	Butts Junction	9 1			9 10			12 3		...	...		3 13		5 49		7 7		10 53		8 23
		Aft. No.1 Up		Aft. No.1 Up		Aft.No.1 Up		Aft.No.2 Up				Aft.No.5 Up		Aft.No.6 Up		Aft.No.8 Up		Aft.No.1 Up		Aft.No.2 Up	
50 44	Faringdon Goods	...	...	9 18	9 28	...	...	...	...	...	...	...	...	...	...	...	...	...	...	...	...
52 24	Tisted	9 8	9 9	9 35	9 50	11 20	11 24	12 10	12 11	...	...	3 19	3 20	5 56	5 57	7 14	7 15	10 59	11 0	8 29	8 30
						Cross No. 2 Up.															
55 27	Privett	9 15	9 16	9 58	10 13	11 30	11 31	12 17	12 18	...	...	3 26	3 27	6 3	6 4	7 21	7 26	11 6	11 7	8 36	8 37
								Cross No. 4 Up.						Cross No. 8 Up.		Cross No. 9 Up.					
59 45	West Meon	9 22	9 23	10 22	10 37	11 37	11 38	12 24	12 26	...	...	3 33	3 34	6 10	6 11	7 32	7 33	11 13	11 14	8 43	8 44
																Cross No.7 Up.					
63 33	Droxford	9 29	9 30	10 46	11 6	11 44	11 45	12 32	12 33	...	...	3 40	3 41	6 17	6 18	7 39	7 40	11 20	11 21	8 50	8 51
				Cross No.2 Up.										CrossNo.7Up							
66 48	Mislingford Gds.	...	...	11 14	11 21	...	...	...	...	...	...	...	...	...	...	...	...	...	...	...	...
68 63	Wickham	9 37	9 38	11 26	12 A2	11 52	11 53	12 40	12 41	...	2 C20	3 48	3 49	6 25	6 26	7 47	7 48	11 28	11 29	8 58	8 59
				Cross No 4 Up. Fol.No. 8 Down.				Pass No.2 Dn. & cross No. 6 Up.													
70 24	Knowle Box		9 42	12 7	12 8		11 56		12 44		2 23		3 52		6 29		7 51		11 32		9 2
70 43	Knowle Platform	9 43	9 44	12 10	12 A20	...	...	12 45	12 46	2 C24	2 30	...	...	...	...	...	...	...	...	...	...
70 50	Fontley Siding	...	...	12 23	12 A33	...	...	...	...	...	...	...	...	...	...	...	...	...	...	...	...
71 39	Fareham	9 48	...	1237	...	12 1	...	1250	...	2 34	2 42	3 57	...	6 34	6 43	7 56 7 58		1137 1140	9	7 9 10
73 56	Fort Brockhurst	...	...	...	...	...	...	...	...	...	...	...	...	6 49	6 50	4 8	5	...	...	...	...
76 20	Gosport	...	...	...	...	...	...	...	...	...	...	...	...	6 53	...	8 8		...	...	...	...

A This Train will take loaded Wagons from Wickham to Knowle Siding, and Empty Wagons from Wickham to Fontley Siding, and loaded wagons from Fontley Siding, and Empty Wagons from Knowle Siding to Fareham.
B Runs last Wednesday in each month and is an Empty Train from Knowle Platform to Wickham.
C Empty Wickham to Knowle Platform, thence Passenger, and runs last Wednesday in each month.
D Stops at Knowle Box to unload Stores on the last day of each month. (T.T. 46,032.)
E Wickham to call over the Train and ascertain if there are any Passengers for the 12.52 p.m. Fareham to Salisbury, and advise Fareham immediately.
F The Station Master at Fareham may order this Train to stop at Knowle Platform on Thursdays when required to take up or set down Passengers from or to the Hants Asylum. (T.T. 38,800.)
G The Station Master at Wickham may order this Train to stop at Knowle Platform on Thursdays when required to set down or take up Passengers to or from the Hants Asylum. (T.T. 38,800.)

Left The 1909 summer timetable for the Meon Valley line, from which it can be seen that the journey times to London (Waterloo) were quite attractive for that era. *Denis Tillman collection*

Right Drummond Class 'T9' 4-4-0 No 30310 trundles through Wickham station with a goods from Mislingford sidings. Note the vegetation on the platforms at a location that was probably the busiest intermediate station on the line; until 1926 it had a footbridge. Following extreme vandalism after closure, the station was demolished in 1971. Today it is just possible to discern the site of the goods yard. *Denis Callender*

Below right An early 1980s view of Droxford station, showing the substantial buildings that still survive. The site was at one time used as a base for training lorry drivers, but is nowadays a very private residence; even when walking the route of the former line, it is almost impossible to catch a glimpse of the station since at this point the walk is diverted away from the trackbed. There used to be two lengthy sidings, cattle dock, crane, goods shed and head shunt here, and until 1914 it was the venue for special trains arriving for Droxford races. *Richard G. Hardy*

Bottom Probably the Meon Valley line's main claim to fame is commemorated by this plaque (not the original), adorning the pillar box at Droxford station. Winston Churchill, General Eisenhower and others spent several days in carriages stabled at this station and at SHAEF headquarters at Southwick formulating the plans for the D-Day invasion. Indeed, a photograph of Winston Churchill and others reputedly at this station used to hang in the booking hall, but closer examination shows a different station canopy design. It is worth noting that around this time our American allies were keen to build a short branch line into the hills near Southwick. *Eddie Rooke*

Bottom right Photographed in October 1996, this loading gauge serves as a reminder of the two sidings that lasted at Mislingford until 1962, one serving the Meon Valley Timber Company and the other a public siding for local farming businesses. The remains of a loading crane still exist today in the undergrowth to the left of this view. *Eddie Rooke*

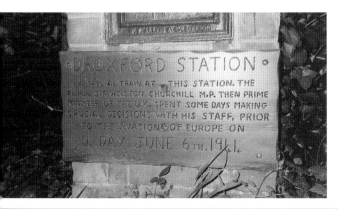

Left Shortly before closure, on Sunday 23 January 1955, Class 'D1' 4-4-0 No 31739 hauled a ramblers' excursion - the 'West Meon Meteor' - from Waterloo, pictured here at West Meon station. This station had the only water columns between Fareham and Alton. Although it boasted living accommodation, the station unfortunately did not possess an electricity supply and therefore failed to attract would-be purchasers after closure. The station buildings were allowed to deteriorate and, aided by continual vandalism, a decision was made to demolish them. The goods yard was used for a while by Hampshire County Council. Today the 600-foot platforms can still be found in heavy undergrowth near the start of the northern end of the Meon Valley railway line walk. *Lens of Sutton*

Below left Demolition of the West Meon viaduct under way in 1956. Some 700 tons of scrap metal were retrieved, and during the dismantling it was discovered that rust was taking a firm grip in places, which could have been a reason for even earlier closure had the decision not been made in 1955. Today the concrete pillars can still be located. *R. K. Blencowe collection*

Top right A 1996 view of Privett station looking across what was previously the goods yard. The buildings are now a private residence and once had the luxury of a fish pond in the space between the two platforms! Apart from the canopy supports still extant on the platform, there is now little to indicate that this was once a railway station. *Eddie Rooke*

Middle right Tisted station in the summer of 1996, viewed from the road bridge. Now in private ownership, railway tracks have been laid to accommodate a saddle-tank steam locomotive currently being overhauled beneath the road bridge. Unfortunately, however, the engine is unlikely to roam too far since houses have been built at one end of the site, while the cutting beyond the road bridge has been filled in. The goods yard was situated between the bridge and the rear of the station buildings. *Eddie Rooke*

Bottom right Following closure to freight trains, the line from Knowle to Droxford was leased to Charles Ashby, who conducted trials with his 'Pace-railer', a single-ended luxury coach that was mounted on four wheels and boasted air-conditioning and reclining seats. It had been hoped to use similar vehicles on the Isle of Wight and other picturesque routes, but the vehicle was severely vandalised, ending the experiment, but not before Mr Ashby had also acquired 'Terrier' tank engine No 32646 (see page 78) and a Maunsell-designed coach for comparison purposes. The station at Droxford was also host to the Southern Locomotive Preservation Company until late 1969; they stored several items of stock there including Class 'USA' 0-6-0 tank engine No 30064, which was subsequently to take up residence on the Bluebell Railway. *Michael G. Harvey*

7.
MISCELLANEOUS RAILWAYS

During the period covered by this book many minor lines of varying gauges existed in the Portsmouth area, some for relatively short periods. Although our research has turned up a great number of such systems, undoubtedly more existed, but hopefully the following examples demonstrate the abundance of railways, other than the national system, that existed at one time.

Because of the area's position on the South Coast, miniature railways at the seaside resorts for the entertainment of children were, at one time, quite commonplace. However, today only one such system remains, but this is situated within a holiday camp and is not open to the general public. The **East Hayling Light Railway** consists of 1 mile of 2-foot-gauge track in a pear-shaped loop (although called 'miniature', this gauge is officially 'narrow'). The station at the start and end of the railway is named Loston Bodged. Locomotives consist of a 1988 Alan Keef-built 0-4-0, which is a steam outline diesel, and another 0-4-0 of 1937, built by Motor Rail, which is a diesel-mechanical. In early 1997 a saddle-tank steam locomotive was under construction.

Carriage stock is interesting, in that one vehicle, a 'toast-rack' type, is from the former Margate Tunnel Railway and is at present 'on loan' from the Hampshire

East Hayling Light Railway: The Alan Keef-built 0-4-0 hauls the very first train in February 1996. *Dave Watson*

Narrow Gauge Railway. Other coaching stock includes three four-wheeled enclosed carriages.

The East Hayling Light Railway is the brain-child of Portsmouth man Mr Bob Haddock, whose bookshop 'Bookstack' in Cosham High Street is well known to local railway enthusiasts for its excellent stock of railway books. Future plans to run a similar railway along Hayling Island sea-front are under discussion.

Prior to the building of the Sea-life Centre in the 1980s, Southsea had its own system in the form of the **Southsea Miniature Railway**, which was situated on the sea-front in close proximity to Southsea Castle. Initially opened as a 9½-inch-gauge layout by Portsmouth Corporation in 1924, the line was taken over after the Second World War by Southsea Miniature Railways Limited who increased the gauge to 10¼ inches. The railway was almost three-quarters of a mile in length and possessed great character - it boasted a turntable, engine shed, tunnel and two 4-4-2 steam locomotives, *Victory* and *Valiant*, until they were displaced by diesels in the final years of the line.

To the north of the city at Hilsea Lido, the **Hilsea Miniature Railway** operated between 1946 and 1950 under the ownership of the late Leonard Baker. The line ran alongside the boating lake from a position close by the swimming pool and gave a round trip of about a mile behind a 4-6-2 steam engine named *Robin Hood*, which was based on an LNER Class 'A1'. This locomotive still survives today in the North of England. The railway had a turntable at each end of the line, an engine shed and a station, of which remains of the platform can still be seen today.

Today the Portsmouth Model Engineering Society operates the **Bransbury Park Railway**, a dual-gauge miniature railway at Bransbury Park in the Milton area of Portsmouth. The gauges are 3½ and 5 inches and the kidney-shaped track is 703 feet long, with a maximum height from the ground of 2 feet. Steam locomotives of both gauges are plentiful; in fact, there are 20 in all, including one diesel and one electric.

The Society was founded in 1946 and originally incorporated model boats, cars and aircraft, but these activities gradually broke away to form their own successful clubs. One of the founder members, Frank Morley, still takes an active part in the running of the railway - over 50 years since its inception!

The Bransbury Park Railway was formally opened in 1977, and the public can travel on the trains, which normally operate every Sunday afternoon during the summer period. A complete renewal of the track and its supports was made in 1993 at a cost of £1,500, funded in part by Portsmouth City Council whose grant of £750 was most gratefully appreciated by the Society.

Southsea Miniature Railway: One of the two 'Atlantic' steam locomotives at the terminus station, attracting quite a crowd of onlookers. Note the fare - only 3d return. *Lens of Sutton*

Left Hilsea Miniature Railway: *Robin Hood* awaits its departure from alongside the boating lake on its round trip of nearly a mile. The carriages are crammed full of excited children. *Roy Baker collection*

Below left Bransbury Park Railway: This GWR 5-inch-gauge 4-6-2 steam locomotive, No 111 *The Great Bear*, is believed to be the only version of this 'Pacific' engine in existence. The driver in this summer 1993 view is Ken Woodroofe, probably better known as an ex-Director on the Mid-Hants Railway Preservation Society (the Watercress Line). *Michael G. Harvey*

Ex-Fratton steam locomotive fireman George Blakey is just one of the many drivers on the railway. His favourite 5-inch-gauge locomotive is Class 'U' 2-6-0 No 31809, carrying a 71D shedplate - George actually drove and fired the prototype in the 1950s when it was allocated to Fratton depot; that one weighed in at 63 tons, but today's model is a mere 2 cwt!

Across the harbour from Portsmouth, the 10½-inch-gauge **Stokes Bay Miniature Railway** commenced operations in 1948 under the ownership of Southern Miniature Railways Limited, who also had sites in Bognor and Poole. The railway started off near the sailing club and formed a long loop, taking in the adjacent paddling-pool area. Unfortunately it was a short-lived line, closing early in the 1950 season amid many objections that its presence spoiled the views across The Solent to the Isle of Wight!

While in the Gosport area, mention must be made of the following other short-lived railways. The **Stokes Bay Light Railway** was of 2-foot gauge in the 1880s, but was later increased to 2 ft 6 in. Initially it connected the pier to the forts at Gilkicker, Monckton and Blockhouse, but the line fell into disrepair in the late 1930s and was subsequently removed. Although records of engines that worked the line are scarce, steam locomotives are known to have been used. Today all trace of this railway has disappeared.

Also long since removed is the **Stokes Bay gravel extraction line,** which was a stretch of temporary track sited near the former Stokes Bay pier.

There were two other lines nearby at Haslar. The **Haslar Tramway** was used in the latter part of the last century to transfer patients from their ships via a jetty in Blockhouse Lake to the Royal Naval Hospital and vice versa. It was a most crude method of transport as the patients were conveyed on cart-type wagons, hand-propelled or horse-drawn! The **Haslar Yacht Marina line** was a temporary short section of narrow gauge railway laid in the 1990s near Haslar Bridge to assist in the construction of the yacht marina.

Just over 40 years earlier the **Bridgemary narrow gauge railway** was a temporary line used to assist in the building of the Bridgemary housing estate in the northern part of Gosport. Diesel motive power was used.

Returning to Portsmouth, a visit to the **City of Portsmouth Preserved Transport Depot** in Old Portsmouth is worthwhile to see the two ex-Portsdown & Horndean Light Railway trams Nos 5 and 13, the latter being in an advanced stage of restoration. No 13 was built in 1903 and ran until 1935, when the system between Cosham and Horndean was closed; it was then purchased privately for the sum of £5 and used as a summer-house at Clanfield near Portsmouth, where it remained until 1973 when it was acquired by Portsmouth City Museums. Its restoration included replacing its upper deck and electric equipment, which had been removed prior to its move to Clanfield; this began in 1992 at the Broad Street depot.

A few hundred yards away from the site of the Bransbury Park Railway is **Eastney Pumping Station**, within which a length of standard gauge railway track once existed.

At **Hilsea Gas Works**, in addition to the standard gauge system, a 2 ft 6 in gauge railway also existed, as did a 2-foot-gauge track nearby, which was used in the construction of the **City Airport** that Portsmouth once had. Also in the same vicinity a private brickyard, in what is now the Claybank and Kiln Roads area (note the brick connections), also had its own narrow gauge track.

Coming out of the city, **Farlington water reservoir** at one time had half a mile of narrow gauge track, the remains of which can still be seen today.

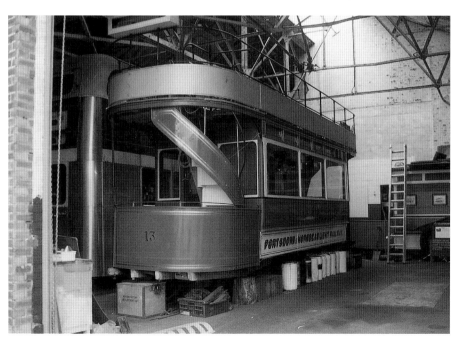

City of Portsmouth Preserved Transport Depot: Portsdown & Horndean Light Railway tram No 13 under restoration in the summer of 1996. *David L. Norman*

At nearby Hayling Island, another brickworks situated within **Pycroft's brickfield** also had a short length of narrow gauge track along which wagons were pushed by hand.

North of Portsmouth, along the former route of the Portsdown & Horndean Light Railway, is situated **J. F. Goodwillie Ltd**, timber merchants and sawmillers since 1882. Although there has never been a railway as such at these premises, the proprietors have kindly provided details of three lengths of track (two utilising hand-pushed trolleys and the other, still in use today, of 5 ft 1½ in gauge, which is powered by a winch). This company did in fact have a railway connection since, in the latter half of the last century, it rented a siding in the Naval Victualling Yard at Gosport for its timber deliveries.

Moving southwards to Portchester, it is not widely known that **Portchester Castle** once had a length of track running along its foreshore, the remains of which were still visible in the early 1950s. Close by, a mineral tramway was laid from Paulsgrove chalk pit, passing under the double-track Cosham to Fareham main lines to reach **Paulsgrove Quay** near today's Port Solent. The chalk was used in the construction of the Western Road at Cosham and also sent to a cement mill in the Isle of Wight.

Not a railway, but worthy of a note in this chapter, is the scrapyard, owned by **Sullivan's**, situated in an old chalk pit at Portsdown Hill Road, Bedhampton (now the site of Sainsbury's Homebase store and a bowling alley). Here a number of ex-Portsmouth Royal Naval Dockyard steam and diesel locomotives were cut up for scrap. Another similar site was **John Pound's Scrapyard** at Tipner, Portsmouth, which although specialising in ship-breaking, was known to have disposed of some BR diesel locomotives in the 1980s.

A local tank engine that escaped the scrapyard but is now preserved away from the Portsmouth area is a Peckett 0-4-0 saddle tank, works No 2100. This 1949-built locomotive originally worked at Hilsea Gas Works and is owned by the City of Portsmouth Museum. Today it is at the Southall Railway Centre in West London.

As can be seen, over the last 150 years there has been a considerable mixture of railways in the Portsmouth area. Regrettably few of the aforementioned installations exist today, in common with other tracks and lines in the area of which there is little knowledge, such as the short lengths of track on **Horsea Island** (probably used for transporting munitions and torpedo testing) and the mill at **Bedhampton**.

Southall Railway Centre: Owned by Portsmouth City Museum and now named *William Murdoch,* this Peckett 0-4-0 saddle tank is pictured in 1995 at work at the Southall Railway Centre. In the summer of 1997 its future was somewhat insecure because of the imminent closure of the Centre following difficulties with the lease. *Michael G. Harvey*

Sullivan's: Four ex-Portsmouth Royal Naval Dockyard steam locomotives await their turn to be scrapped at the premises of Southern Counties Demolition (Sullivan's) in Bedhampton. Left to right, the engines are No 15 (Avonside, works No 1659, built 1915), No 10 (Andrew Barclay, works No 2039, built 1937), No 18 (Bagnall, works No 2602, built 1938), and No 14 (Avonside, works No 1658, built 1915). Pictured in April 1961. *Bruce Oliver*

8.
SUCCESSORS TO STEAM

Text, photographs and captions by Bruce Oliver

It is fortunate that railways did not die with the demise of the steam locomotive, otherwise the most agreeable method of land transport would now be denied to us, and this would be an enormous loss. Indeed, rail travel since the age of steam has advanced impressively. Trains are now invariably clean, quick, smooth and quiet, while timetables complement these improvements with the convenience of regular-interval services. Upholstery for the passenger may lack the sumptuous appointments of pre-nationalisation conditions, but the overall benefits outweigh any minor criticism.

Portsmouth was most fortunate in being an early candidate for electrification, July 1937 marking the transition to a new experience. Apart from suburban electrification schemes, which had been extended progressively since before the First World War, it was the Southern Railway under Sir Herbert Walker that saw the advantages and economy in main-line electrification. The LBSCR had introduced an overhead system for suburban lines, but this was superseded during the 1920s by the present, rugged, third-rail feed. The LSWR, meanwhile, had started its own suburban electrification with third rail, a method later to be adopted for the whole of the Southern. Brighton, Worthing and Eastbourne were the first targets for main-line electrification during the 1930s, but Portsmouth managed to get in on the act just prior to the outbreak of war. The former LSWR main line via Guildford was converted in 1937, with the former LBSCR route via Horsham following a year later; this latter scheme also provided Bognor Regis as another electrified terminus.

Dedicated new builds of stock were allocated to these conversions:

Fast trains
4COR/4RES/4COR for 12-car fast trains, Waterloo-Portsmouth.
4COR/4BUF/4COR for 12-car fast trains, Victoria-Bognor Regis and Portsmouth (4COR detached/attached at Barnham for Portsmouth).

Slow trains
2BIL, augmented by 2NOL and, later, 2HAL for 2/4/6/8-car trains (occasionally 10/12 cars).

These combinations also worked coastal services from Brighton to Portsmouth and Hastings.

The war brought an abrupt halt to both electrification and the building of new lines, with Chessington-Leatherhead being abandoned without resumption. Kent saw the first post-war electrification project, completed in two phases during 1959-61, with Bournemouth following in 1967. Since that time, gaps in the system have been progressively plugged, with the long overdue section between Portsmouth and Southampton/Eastleigh coming live in 1990.

The electrified lines into Portsmouth received no new stock until 1963, when, for a very brief period, a small batch of production 4CEP units, the last to be built, operated peak-period 12-car formations from Waterloo. The prototype 4CEP/BEP units, 7101-04 and 7001/02, did operate from Victoria to Bognor Regis in the late 1950s, so an occasional modern unit used to appear in Portsmouth at that time, but with no guaranteed regularity.

The first replacement scheme for Southern main-line stock came in 1965, when the Brighton units (6PUL and 6PAN) were edged out by the first batch of 4CIG/BIG units. These units later began to appear in Portsmouth, meeting compatibility demands with Bognor Regis formations. At this time random 4CEP units started to appear on coastal services between Portsmouth and Brighton, units constructed originally for Kent, whither they had returned by the early 1970s.

It was the Bournemouth electrification of 1967 that issued the first major threat to the traditional scene in Portsmouth, for it was then that 4VEP units appeared for the first time, offering serious competition as much with the interim measure of older 2HAP units as with the 30-year-old 2BIL/HAL stock. 2HAP units, constructed

4COR unit 3152 leads a 12-car formation at Portsmouth Harbour, awaiting departure on a fast service to Waterloo on 3 October 1965. With the most recent structural restoration at this station, the outer platform (No 5) survives in use, while platform 2 has been closed.

upon the frames of the 2NOL units (all having been withdrawn a decade or more earlier), had, from the mid-1960s, shared services with the BIL/HAL stock, though electrically incompatible. Following the Bournemouth batch of 4VEP units (7701-20), the build continued relentlessly through to unit 7894. After Bournemouth's allocation came Brighton's first delivery, with further batches going to ex-LSWR main-line services, as well as to Kent.

Thus the era of the 2BIL/HAL came to an end in Portsmouth in July 1971. During June 1970 Portsmouth received its first allocation from the new build of 4CIG/BIG stock. While the Brighton units of 1965 represented the very peak of travelling comfort on the Southern - deep cushions, padded arm rests, winged seating, etc - the new batch of 4CIGs provided a very mean environment by comparison, being no match for the 4COR units that they were to displace. The bouncy ride afforded by 4COR stock was all part of the experience, and quite thrilling in its way. The comparative smoothness of the new 4CIG stock only

served to turn one's attention to the sheer boredom of the internal appointments and the hardness of the upholstery.

The final main-line turn by a rake of 4COR stock occurred on 5 October 1970, though the units lingered for a while on coastal services to Brighton. It should be mentioned that the original 4RES units of 1937 were modernised during the 1950s and 1960s to provide buffet and griddle vehicles (4GRI).

During the 1960s 2HAP units of Bulleid profile appeared on services into Portsmouth and, as the years rolled on, 2HAP units from the 1959/61 Kent builds joined existing HAP and VEP stock on both coastal and Waterloo services. In their final years large numbers of 2HAP units were joined in semi-permanent pairs to form 4CAP units and, in this form, operation on Brighton-Portsmouth services continued for some time.

Unit classes have experienced several changes of identity over the years, both in livery and numbering. The CIGs began life in the 73XX and 74XX series, changing finally to 17XX, 18XX and 13XX in the 1990s. Similarly, VEPs began life as 77XX and 78XX, metamorphosing through 30XX and 31XX to their present refurbished form as 34XX and 35XX. The glorious tradition of all-over green for Southern multiple units gave way during the late 1960s to the drab, dirty corporate image of dull blue, with the tasteless addition of white vinyl stick-on numbers. This dreary uniform soon yielded to the improved blue/grey livery, though still noticeably inferior to the dignified and thoroughly self-confident image traditionally associated with the Southern. The 4CIG units began life in association with 4BIG units, where buffet facilities were provided, but these units were superseded by refurbished 4BEP units from Kent during the 1980s.

Chris Green, Managing Director of the newly formed Network SouthEast, brought a new sense of purpose to rail transport, along with a new, startling livery. Brash it may have been, but it did much to put railways back in the forefront of good business practice. Critics had a nit-picking field day, but the benefits slowly demolished initial opposition. The introduction of the Network Card positively encouraged rail travel over a very wide area, going well beyond places normally associated with the South East.

Mr Green's masterpiece has to be the new breed of main-line stock. The Class 442 units, initially built for Bournemouth, eventually came to operate Portsmouth services, and are now as much a feature of the main line via Guildford as they are of their original dedicated route. The absence of route code boxes is a disadvantage to the observer, but this is a matter that may be corrected with the passage of time. This might be perceived as a touch of nit-picking by the writer himself.

Uncommon units in Portsmouth over the years have been those specifically built for other services. The 6PUL/PAN/CIT stock, built for the Brighton main-line scheme of the early 1930s, rarely visited Portsmouth, but appear they did from time to time on specials, as did the

Summary of motive power referred to in this chapter

Electric multiple units

SUB: General suffix for all pre-EPB suburban units of SR origin.

EPB: General suffix applied to all 2- and 4-car suburban stock fitted with electro-pneumatic braking.

2BIL: 2-car corridor, non-gangwayed semi-fast units.

2HAL: 2-car semi-fast units, with one non-corridor vehicle.

2HAP: 2-car non-gangwayed semi-fast units.

2NOL: 2-car non-corridor 'suburban' units, converted from LSWR steam stock.

4BEP: 4-car gangwayed express units, including a buffet car, refurbished ex-Kent 1959/61 builds. Buffet cars subsequently running out of use.

4BIG: 4-car gangwayed express units, including a buffet car.

4BUF: 4-car corridor, gangwayed express units with buffet car.

4CEP: 4-car gangwayed express units, delivered in quantity for Kent in 1959/61.

4CIG: 4-car gangwayed express units.

4COR: 4-car corridor, gangwayed express units.

4LAV: 4-car non-gangwayed semi-fast units for the Brighton scheme.

4RES: 4-car corridor, gangwayed express units with restaurant car.

4VEP: 4-car gangwayed semi-fast units, with doors to each bay/compartment.

5BEL: 5-car internally gangwayed all-Pullman units for the 'Brighton Belle'.

6PUL/PAN/CIT: 6-car internally gangwayed express units for Brighton/Eastbourne/Worthing.

4TC: Trailer unit - 4-car gangwayed non-motor units, compatible with Bournemouth 4REP units, Class 33 diesel and Class 73 electro-diesel locomotives, for push-pull working.

Class 319: 4-car internally gangwayed units for both suburban and main-line use.

Class 442: 5-car gangwayed express units, incorporating a buffet car. Sometimes referred to as 5WES. Electrical equipment from withdrawn 4REP units.

Class 455: 4-car gangwayed suburban units.

Class 456: 2-car internally gangwayed suburban units.

Diesel multiple units ('Sprinters')

All units are gangwayed.

Class 150: 2-car second-generation units, gangwayed and internally gangwayed types.

Class 155: 2-car second-generation units, later withdrawn and rebuilt as single-car units, redesignated Class 153. Transferred for use elsewhere.

Class 156: 2-car second-generation units, later transferred for use elsewhere.

Class 158: Basically 2-car second-generation 'Super Sprinters'.

Class 159: Purpose-built 3-car 'Super Sprinters' for Network SouthEast.

Hastings units: 6-car internally gangwayed units, from three builds: short units, long units and buffet-car units (6S, 6L and 6B, later Classes 201/2/3).

all-Pullman 5BEL units. The 4LAV units, built for semi-fast services in the Brighton scheme, managed occasional diagrammed workings into Portsmouth. There was, for example, a brief period when they appeared regularly on a Friday evening service from London Bridge. Summer Saturdays and weekday peak periods used to entice 4SUB units beyond their own dedicated territory, when available stock of any age might appear on a 'visit to the seaside'.

It should be noted that, until the arrival of EPB stock in the 1950s, all existing Southern units shared compatible electrical equipment, and couplings of different classes took place, irrespective of gearing. More recently 4EPB units appeared from time to time, in the tradition of sending suburban units to the coast for a change of air. Encouragement of this practice was prompted originally by the introduction of 2HAP units on stopping services from London, where electrical compatibility existed. Even so, visits were rare.

During the 1970s/'80s, the initial build for the Bournemouth electrification of 1967, classified 4REP and 4TC, made unavoidable visits, when engineering works put the main line through Winchester out of action at weekends. Before electrification of Portsmouth-Southampton, these diversions were towed by Class 33 diesel locomotives either direct to Havant, or into and out of Portsmouth. The 4TC units did eventually form services to Portsmouth in their own right, when, with a Class 33 as motive power, they briefly operated services to and from Reading.

Modern suburban units have made appearances in Portsmouth, including the Thameslink Class 319s. With the restoration of Fratton as a maintenance depot, units of Classes 455 and 456 have appeared for modification by Fratton staff. A Class 455 is even rumoured to have appeared in service locally.

Meanwhile, electric and electro-diesel locomotives have always been seen in the area. The original Southern locomotives (Nos 20001/2/3) used to appear on freight workings and occasional specials, while during a short spell in the early 1960s they became regular daily visitors on the Brighton-Portsmouth section of the through service from Brighton to Plymouth. The Class 73 electro-diesels have by now achieved a long and reliable record of service, being seen in Portsmouth upon a variety of tasks over many years. More recently their activities

A push-pull-fitted Class 33, together with a 4TC unit, backs into the siding at Blackfriars Junction to allow other train movements to proceed in and out of the Low Level platforms on 5 April 1987, a day when the High Level was temporarily out of use. The new signalling centre is shown on the site of the former turntable and locomotive servicing point.

have been limited to engineering works trains. One such locomotive, No 73130, was named *City of Portsmouth* in 1988, but with the need for locomotives to serve specific callings these days, the names have been removed. There remains one outstanding omission from the list at this point, this being London Transport's No 12 *Sarah Siddons*. This splendid machine has been allowed out into the country on several occasions since being passed fit for main-line service, and Portsmouth first hosted such a visit on 7 July 1984.

Diesel locomotives first appeared in the Portsmouth area with the arrival of the 152XX series shunters in the 1950s. Not long afterwards these non-standard machines were replaced by the since ubiquitous Class 08. Examples of this class remained until Fratton no longer serviced freight traffic, their duties having included the Dockyard goods diagram. When the first series of main-line locomotives, built exclusively for operation over Southern Region territory, arrived in the early 1960s, examples of the class (Class 33) visited Portsmouth only rarely, surviving non-electrified locomotive-hauled services employing steam power until displacement by Western Region D70XX (Class 35) locomotives during the late 1960s. These 'Hymek' locomotives lasted on Bristol/Cardiff services until their non-standard credentials necessitated early withdrawal during the 1970s. The 'Hymeks' were in turn replaced by Class 31s, an extensive class that had by then spread its members far beyond its Eastern Region origins.

No 20002 at Portsmouth Harbour on 31 March 1965, about to convey HM The Queen to Waterloo via Guildford. The station was rebuilt for the electrification scheme of 1937.

The Bristol/Cardiff services are now operated by Class 158 units almost exclusively, but until their introduction the Southern's own Class 33 locomotives performed usefully on these services, following the changeover from Class 31. Before the 'Sprinter' era, Class 47s did, however, achieve a diagram on these services, if only briefly. It should be noted that a Class 31, No D5621, visited Portsmouth in 1961 on an excursion from North London, years before the Western Region allocation.

The introduction of Class 158s on cross-country services was not the first such use of diesel multiple units on these diagrams as, during the previous quarter-century, both Hampshire units (diesel-electric) and WR units (diesel-mechanical) had been employed on inter-regional operations between Portsmouth and Bristol/South Wales.

Prior to the introduction of the Class 158 units most recently, there was a short period during which units of Classes 155 and 156 operated the services to and from the former Western Region. Occasionally, examples of the humbler Class 150 series have appeared, as a result of stock shortages. Network SouthEast's very own Class 159s, a three-car variation of the Class 158, operate diagrams into Portsmouth and along the coast (as well as Waterloo-Southampton shuttles), though they were originally built specifically for the Waterloo-Exeter services.

Historically, diesel multiple units arrived upon the scene in Portsmouth with a vengeance in 1957, when services to Southampton, Eastleigh, Salisbury and, eventually, Andover were operated on a regular-interval timetable with the new Hampshire units (since Class 205). Very soon these units were temporarily withdrawn in order that they might receive improved silencing

Above In March 1972 'Hymek' No 7038 enters Portsmouth & Southsea on a service from the Western Region. These trains, normally comprising five vehicles at the time, usually featured a Full Brake ('BG') in the formation, rather than a 'BSK'. The 'BG', here shown as an outer vehicle, often appeared in the centre of the train.

Below Nos 37250 and D9000 *Royal Scots Grey* on exhibition at Portsmouth & Southsea during a special events day on 2 July 1988, when No 73130 was named *City of Portsmouth* and 4SUB 4732, coupled to 2BIL 2090, operated local shuttles. The High Level station was rebuilt between 13 February and 25 March 1988; the reduced arrangement had been established in the early spring of 1985, when the two surviving platforms became 3 and 4, while the High Level through platforms (formerly 6 and 7) became 1 and 2. No 37250 is seen here at the former platform 5.

No 47547, deputising for a Class 50, is on a Portsmouth Harbour to Waterloo service in July 1989 during the period when Class 50s were employed on a triangular Exeter-Portsmouth-Waterloo diagram. The train is seen descending from the High Level station. The new 'Do It All' store, standing on the site of the original platforms 1-3, can be seen to the right of the picture.

equipment, so steam returned briefly. But these units have since proved very reliable and sturdy, their use on the Southern being finally restricted to the Uckfield stump. In their time they worked to Reading and along the Bournemouth and Exeter main lines, with workings into Waterloo from time to time. As mentioned above, they even operated regular services for a while beyond Salisbury, over the former GWR line to Bristol. Final rites for the Winchester-Alton service were entrusted to the units, before preservation took hold upon Alresford. They officially ceased to be diagrammed into Portsmouth with the electrification of the links to Eastleigh and Southampton in 1990.

It is worthy of note that the initial 1957 batch was soon expanded from two-car to three-car units, with the addition of a non-driving trailer, indicating the popularity of the services offered. The initial batch of 1957 (Nos 1101-1126) was later augmented by a further smaller order in 1963, when deliveries extended the class to unit No 1133. Alterations and movement of units within the Southern Region occurred as the years passed, but the most significant change locally was the insertion of former electric multiple unit driving trailers (with equipment stripped) in four of the class, creating four hybrid units, numbered 1401-04. Four of the original batch (1119-22) had not been expanded to three-car units when the rest were so modified, their use having been initially confined to Ashford-Hastings services.

Since electrification on the lines west of Portsmouth, services have been dominated predictably by 4VEP and 4CIG units, with some services now extending from Brighton through to Bournemouth, Basingstoke and Waterloo, using the Portsmouth avoiding line between Farlington and Cosham. Services between Portsmouth and Waterloo via Eastleigh commenced with electrification, but were later withdrawn, only to be replaced later by a limited service at peak periods, though this has subsequently been altered again to include a limited through service during the day. The situation seems to be subject to constant change.

Prior to electrification, Class 33 locomotives, powering 4TC stock, operated services to Basingstoke and Reading for a while. These versatile locomotives also appeared regularly for some time on the through Brighton-Exeter workings, when pairs

of Class 33s operated in tandem. These operations had superseded the earlier, interesting diagrams, when 12-car trains were seen, employing pairs of Hastings units (10XX series) for these Saturday services. Latterly, Hastings units appeared on special workings from time to time, when impromptu visits to the Portsmouth area occurred.

The larger main-line diesel locomotives have never had very much to do with Portsmouth, though members of Class 47 have inevitably appeared on long-distance summer services more than any other class. For a while Classes 45/46 used to appear on Saturday services to Leeds or Sheffield. More recently Class 37s have become established, with allocation of members to the Southern reflecting the demise of the Class 33. Even so, their visits are rare, usually involving engineering works. The Western Region's Classes 42 and 52 locomotives registered visits to the Portsmouth area in their time, generally on as-required aggregate diagrams to destinations in Sussex. More recently Class 59s have made their debut.

A brief period of excitement was provided during the 1980s, when the need to make better use of the Class 50s on the Waterloo-Exeter services involved an operation into Portsmouth, followed by a run up the Direct Line to Waterloo during the afternoon. A similar reverse service operated down to Portsmouth during the morning period. The Direct Line certainly provided a most interesting testing ground for the 50s' capabilities, while enthusiasts were not short of something attractive to sample, if only for a limited period.

The diesel fuelling point at Fratton, alongside platform 3, exists as it has done since its construction in 1961. Open to the elements, servicing of diesel operation in Portsmouth remains a very inhospitable task, no doubt emphasising the secondary nature of such motive power in a city that has been especially associated with electrification since before the Second World War.

On 11 April 1988 No 50001 *Dreadnought* **brings a Waterloo to Portsmouth Harbour service along the continuous embankment between Portsmouth & Southsea and Portsmouth Harbour. This link to the Harbour station, known as the Portsmouth Joint Extension Railway, dates from 1876.**

Above D137 *The Cheshire Regiment*, in charge of the Saturdays-only Portsmouth Harbour to Leeds service, is seen passing Fratton in August 1968. The Thompson vehicle next to the locomotive is worthy of note.

Below 2BIL 2029 leads another of the class on a Brighton to Portsmouth Harbour semi-fast service in June 1970. Fratton station is in the background, where a 2HAL unit can be seen on an up service at platform 1. Beyond the footbridge a 4COR unit can just be seen, stored in a non-electrified siding in the goods yard, while one of the new-generation 4VEP units is parked on the nearside route into the carriage shed on the right, following the path of the erstwhile East Southsea branch.

London Transport No 12 *Sarah Siddons* stands with its stock alongside platform 3 at Fratton on 7 July 1984, on the occasion of its visit to Portsmouth. The attendant Class 47 is seen in one of the adjacent through lines. In the background can be seen the diesel fuelling point, built in 1961, with a Hampshire diesel unit in attendance.

Beyond the Class 47 one of the Southern Region's de-icing units is stored; these units generally comprised the withdrawn motor driving vehicles from 4SUB units, with modernised cab ends. Fratton yard in the distance then contained large numbers of withdrawn vans.

Above A view of Fratton up platform, with hybrid 4CAP unit 3303 working a stopping service to Brighton on 5 May 1984. The reduced awning on the down island platform is evident, as is the truncated roofing to the footbridge. The station dates from the East Southsea branch opening in 1885.

Below A down Waterloo-Portsmouth fast passes between Kingston Cemetery and the refurbished Kingston Prison at St Mary's Road Bridge on 22 August 1986. The leading unit is 2307, one of the modernised 4BEP units (2301-07) that displaced the 4BIGs in the 1980s.

Above A Class 73 electro-diesel enters Portsmouth on 27 August 1982 with a mixed rake of wagons from the Chichester/Brighton line (Code 1B). It is seen just south of the Hilsea Gas Works site; the pointwork serving the surviving sidings can just be seen on the right above the trackside concrete structures.

Below A pair of Class 442 units passes the same location on 24 March 1995; by this time, 12½ years later, the gas works connections have long since disappeared. The units are operating a fast service from Waterloo, having by this time become customary stock for such diagrams.

Above Unrebuilt 4BEP 7013 cruises through Hilsea on the 14.50 Portsmouth Harbour to Victoria service on 13 August 1981. At this time two such diagrams a day brought the buffet car unit to Portsmouth, rather than Bognor Regis. The unit will link up at Barnham Junction with 4CIG units from Bognor Regis. Hilsea remains a rudimentary station, though its use has increased significantly in recent years with surrounding commercial development and a residential estate on the site of the former airfield. At one time Hilsea was only served by a few peak-period services; now it receives the recognition of an all-day timetable.

Below 2HAP 6053 leads a 4VEP on a Brighton-Portsmouth semi-fast across Portcreek on 24 June 1978, with the junction for Cosham in the background. The depth of the indicator panel betrays its original use for blinds using numerals of the same size and style as those used for SR metal stencils. The picture is taken from the top of Hilsea Lines, with the then recent A27 road bridge in use over the railway at the junction.

Above   Seen from the opposite direction, No 50020 *Revenge* emerges from Hilsea Lines and crosses Portcreek in August 1987 while operating the afternoon service to Waterloo over the Direct Line via Guildford.

Below   4SUB 4732 and 2BIL 2090 travel between Farlington Junction and Portcreek Junction while working a Southern Electric Group special on 23 March 1984. Both units are operating in preservation.

Above A pair of Class 33 diesels is seen passing Farlington Junction en route to Brighton on the through service from Exeter on 22 August 1981. The former station at Farlington Junction closed, somewhat ironically, with the start of electrified services in 1937.

Below A 4VEP, forming a down stopping service from Waterloo (code 73) in September 1976, is seen travelling along the flat land past Farlington Marshes. The picture is taken at Farlington Junction, with Bedhampton in the far distance. At this point there were sidings on both sides of the line, the down side being a storage point for condemned stock in the early 1960s.

Above On 27 February 1987 4CIG 7420 leads a 12-car rake on a Portsmouth-Waterloo fast through Bedhampton station, a structure providing only the most basic facilities, amounting to little more than the platforms themselves.

Below 4VEP 7844 enters Bedhampton on a down stopping service on 29 May 1982, passing the now vanished signal box. The station at Havant is only 1,162 yards from that at Bedhampton, the latter having opened originally in 1906.

In March 1972, 4CEP 7116, having just left Bedhampton, is approaching Stockheath Crossing on a stopping Brighton service, and will already be preparing to apply the brakes for Havant.

Riding the 4CORs on the Portsmouth Direct Line

Electrification of the Southern Railway main lines brought with it a travelling experience, sufficiently different from that provided by steam trains to earn a position of some distinction. Just as the arrival of High Speed Trains on the Western and Eastern Regions in the 1970s revolutionised services beyond dispute, so did the advances of 40 years earlier by the Southern. Life was never the same again.

Timetables were developed around a reliable interval service, with the trains themselves providing a clean and pleasant environment. Portsmouth received new express units, the 4COR and 4RES series, subsequently always to be associated with the city, even though their use took them elsewhere on the system. The internal carriages were of similar design and atmosphere to vehicles that R. E. L. Maunsell had produced for steam haulage, but the outer vehicles, containing the motor bogies, left one in no doubt that a new age in main-line travel had dawned.

To travel in a motor vehicle - and they constituted two out of the four carriages in every such unit - was always a thrill, provided one did not wish to do anything other than enjoy the experience itself. Perhaps the Southern ought to have issued warnings that anyone wishing to read, or partake of a drink, would only do so at their own risk, as the ride was guaranteed to impose its peculiarities upon the most determined stoic.

As any train of COR/RES stock started to move, there was the initial 'clunk', as the motor bogie attempted to gain distance on the carriage it was supporting. Then followed the growling determination of the motor, proving its ability to accelerate a train as could no steam locomotive.

The open saloons were divided into two sections, with a sliding door that completely sealed one from the other when closed. These used to offer smoking/non-smoking areas, though the connecting door invariably remained open. The walls of the saloons were panelled generously in varnished wood, while the curved ceilings were finished in white gloss paint. The seating was arranged in what one might describe as double arm-chairs - settees, even - with winged head-rests, padded arm-rests and thick upholstered cushions that could be removed with ease. These 'settees' were back-to-back, providing 4-seat bays, with plenty of leg room, in contrast to today's mean appointments. Above the line where the 'settee' backs came together there was a bronzed luggage rack, with an interlaced, curved wire base to support the load. Lighting was ceiling-mounted, with exposed bulbs nesting in small diamond-shaped mirrors. The overall effect was impressive. Seating was numbered by disks screwed to the wall panelling, a practice that was followed for many decades into BR on Mk I stock.

With a journey under way, the experience rapidly began to take hold on the traveller. Rail joints - and they came every 60 feet before long welded rail was invented - provided repetitious music as the 'chink' of the equipment accompanied the continuous, aggressive humming of the bogie-mounted motor. It was truly a powerful experience. Speed had only to reach modest express demands for the COR characteristics to reach sublimation. Rhythm took over and the units would dance to their own music. Up and down, side to side, bouncing all the way to London, the rides were ones of memorable excitement and, for those sensitively initiated, far more rewarding than anything steam could offer.

There were particular points on the journey that became measuring zones, giving rise to that sense of anticipation that one feels for certain passages in a

Beethoven symphony that one has already heard a hundred times before. Portcreek was the first such zone, where the train, now probably exceeding the ruling speed restriction, would chase over the points at an alarming rate. Bags might fall over on the floor here, while adjacent passengers would engage in momentary physical intimacy that might not be desired.

For many years the through roads were used at Havant, when the residential importance of the town and its environs was insufficient to require a stop. Dashing through the station one felt superior, though without any real justification. Probably it was because one delighted in the train's contempt for a platform road. Round the curve to the Direct Line, the units then began to think about the climb to Buriton. Banging their way through the curves and echoes of Rowlands Castle, the task was serious. Beyond milepost 62 the climb began in earnest, with severe curves and a gradient of 1 in 80. Here the motors could be heard working flat out, howling round the bends, with the bogies shaking their components to the steady beat. At last milepost 58¼ came into sight, the summit, and the crazy descent to Petersfield through Buriton Tunnel began.

Speed advanced through the tunnel quite alarmingly, and by the time one reached Petersfield it was often necessary to hold on to anything in sight that appeared reliable, in order that a safe passage might be guaranteed. With a 40-ton motor-bogied vehicle travelling at breakneck speed, lurching from side to side, there was always the feeling that one was about to leave the track, yet such disaster never struck in all the years that the beloved units ran between Portsmouth and Waterloo. No worry really, and far better than a visit to the fun-fair.

In conclusion, one may breach the strict bounds of this book by referring, briefly, to a few other relevant points. In both up and down directions, the COR units provided a sensational experience on the quadruple track down to Woking, where the straight lines allowed all hell to be let loose. Observing the units from a station platform was equally thrilling, for, as they approached, the leading gangway connection oscillated violently from side to side, giving a real sense of energy.

Back inside a train, the desire to walk from carriage to carriage offered a test to the passenger, rarely fulfilled with dignity. Shoulder bruising was not unknown, as one dared to make

progress. Assault upon one's fellow travellers was an accepted feature, usually covered with a smile of shared understanding. Landing upon the laps of others, when passing through an open saloon, was a far from rare occurrence.

Before the days of roller-blinds for route indicators, the units carried boxes for metal stencils in the guard's van. As the guard's van lived over the motor-bogie, the ultimate experience was provided by a sojourn at this point, where the shaking stencils added to the percussion effects quite agreeably.

Claims for speed achievements for the CORs may not be well documented, but to regulars on the line there were frequent occasions when line speed far exceeded the ruling restrictions of the day. In the up direction, the curves approaching Witley invariably initiated a short prayer, though one always survived. In the down direction, the section between Haslemere and Petersfield remains, to this day, the high point of excitement. Countless records of CORs shattering over the level crossing at Liss in excess of 90 mph must exist, with the elusive 100 so nearly touched on many occasions.

Thankfully, the writer can confirm that 100 was exceeded at least once in his experience, when Liss was probably passed at 103 mph. This happy day was 28 February 1968, when the 10.9 miles between Haslemere and Petersfield were covered in little over 9 minutes, start to stop. What would, for decades, have been regarded as exceptional performances became quite regular in the units' last three or four years, right up to their disappearance from the route in October 1970. The writer can express no apology for his personal infatuation with these remarkable units. They combined charm, character and excitement, and should have challenged the reasoning of any supporter of rail travel, still hopelessly attached to the age of steam. Well done, the Southern Railway!

4COR 3129 is seen at Stockheath Crossing (now dismantled) on the same day, working a stopping service from Brighton. This was almost the last appearance of COR stock in Portsmouth, its use on the Direct Line via Guildford having ceased in 1970.

Above A 4VEP approaches Havant on a down stopping service from Waterloo in July 1977. The picture is taken from the site of the Hayling Island branch platform, with the former trackbed by then in use as a bus park for Southdown. Two Leyland PD3s and a Bristol VR are seen at rest, no longer wearing the magnificent Southdown livery of green and cream.

Below 4VEP 7846 leaves Havant from the down platform on an up Waterloo stopping service on 14 March 1981, a day when engineering works prevented rail services continuing west of Havant. The four tracks between the platforms resulted from the station remodelling of the 1930s, in association with electrification.

Above right 4VEP 3035, displaying Network SouthEast livery, leads another of its class away from the west end of Havant station on a down stopping service from Waterloo in August 1991. The up through line had by this time been removed, though the down line remains in use.

Right 4BIG 7051 leads a 4CIG on a down fast service from Waterloo over the junction at Havant in May 1978. The LBSCR main line to Chichester is seen behind the 4BIG, with Warblington Halt just visible in the distance. The Direct Line from Waterloo, opened in 1859, post-dates the LBSCR route by 12 years.

Above Doyen 4COR unit 3101, though not in its original formation, leads another such unit through Rowlands Castle on a down fast service from Waterloo in August 1970. The loading gauge, providing evidence of the former goods yard and now itself redundant, frames the units menacingly, as if to presage their demise over the Direct Line, by this time just six weeks away. The unit exhibits the tedious 'Rail blue' livery.

Below Bulleid-profile 2HAP 5633 coasts down from Buriton at Finchdean heading towards Rowlands Castle on a stopping service on 20 July 1968. The black triangle on the front vehicle indicates that it contains the guard's compartment.

Above A 2HAL, in 'Rail blue' livery, leads a 2BIL from the south end of 485-yard Buriton Tunnel on a down stopping service from Waterloo in August 1969. Until electrification of the line between Basingstoke and Winchester in 1967, the section from Petersfield to Rowlands Castle was, at 8.34 miles, the longest section of electrified line anywhere on the Southern between stations.

Below 4CIG 7345 leads a 12-car rake out of the north end of Buriton Tunnel on an up semi-fast service on 19 April 1985. Evidence of the former engineers' sidings at Buriton can be seen here.

4CIG 7414, one of the final batch of units for the SW Division, is joined by another of the class on a down stopping service from Waterloo to Portsmouth Harbour (code 83) on 19 April 1985. The scene is Idsworth, where the line finally straightens out after the tortuous descent from Buriton Tunnel. The tunnel is just beyond the pylons in the right background of the picture.

Above 4CIG 7354 heads a 12-car train on an up fast to Waterloo from Portsmouth on the descent from Buriton Tunnel on 29 May 1982. The gap between the hills in the background has, in recent times, been greatly widened to serve the needs of the A3 trunk road.

Below An up train of vans from Portsmouth to Clapham, headed by a Class 33 diesel locomotive, descends at speed from Buriton into Petersfield on 20 July 1985. The very end of the up-side siding from the station can be seen to the right of the picture.

On 20 July 1985 Hastings unit 1013 rushes through Petersfield on a down special (SW code 48) jointly for the Southern Electric Group and the Railway Correspondence & Travel Society.

Above 4VEP 7840 enters Petersfield, past the signal box, on a down stopping train from Waterloo on 21 April 1984. The Midhurst branch service used to depart from a platform alongside the buildings seen here behind the 4VEP. The line proceeded under the right-hand arch of the overbridge in the background, before turning sharp right into West Sussex.

Below Now returning to the lines west of Portsmouth, former 'Oxted' unit 207013 (ex-13XX series) runs into Cosham on a Portsmouth to Salisbury service on 31 March 1989. Just prior to electrification a few such units appeared on services out of Portsmouth, following their displacement from East Grinstead by electrification. The earthworks of the former head-shunt on the down side can be seen, now lightly covered in vegetation.

Above Hybrid '3T' unit 1403 enters Cosham from the west, on a service from Reading on 13 June 1981. The signal box was then still open to control the busy crossing, but has since been demolished. The unit displays the full-depth route indicator box, indicating that it was one of the first batch of units, when Southern Railway-style numerals were carried on the blinds.

Below Electro-diesel No 73142 leads another of the class, double-heading a working of the VSOE rake of Pullman cars through Cosham on 16 April 1983. No 73142, named *Broadlands*, was at this time something of a celebrity, being used on many special workings. Note the further use of SW Division special code 48.

Above With Portchester station in the distance, two Class 156 units race along towards Fareham with a Regional Railways service from Portsmouth to South Wales on 27 March 1989. Some of these services have travelled through to Carmarthen and beyond. The Class 156 units did not last long in the area, soon being displaced by Class 158s, the latter at present providing a permanent service.

Below On the same day the last Hampshire unit, by now renumbered 205033, negotiates the single line between Botley and Fareham, and is about to enter the tunnel between Knowle and Fareham. It is operating a service from Reading, only a year or so before electrification of this piece of line, yet there is no evidence of either third rail or insulators by the track.

9.
STEAM RETURNS
TO THE CITY

On 9 July 1967 the last BR steam train departed from Portsmouth, and later the same day the last steam locomotive arrived at Fratton, then departed for Eastleigh 'light engine' for withdrawal. This day also marked the end of the steam locomotive in operational service with the Southern Region of British Railways. The two steam engines mentioned were BR Standard Class '5' 4-6-0 No 73029 with a train of empty passenger stock for Clapham Junction, and Class 'USA' 0-6-0T No 30072 en route from Guildford (where it had been depot pilot) to Eastleigh. This tank was, at a later date, destined to be preserved and used on the Worth Valley Railway in Yorkshire.

One or two projects to run a steam-hauled train to Portsmouth in the early 1990s, involving preserved 'King Arthur' Class 4-6-0 No 777 *Sir Lamiel*, had been frustrated, then it was announced early in 1994 that preserved rebuilt 'Merchant Navy' Class 4-6-2 No 35028 *Clan Line* would head a charter train from London to Portsmouth and return on Saturday 24 September, as a charity fund-raising venture. After running driver training trips between Eastleigh and Yeovil and other runs via Southall and Basingstoke, *Clan Line* carried out a trial run on Saturday 17 September over the same route and to the same timings as the main Portsmouth run projected for the 24th. *Clan Line* steamed out of London (Victoria) at 15.45 with a train of nine InterCity coaches and a support coach, and with Class 47 diesel No 47770 *Reserve* in red livery coupled to the rear to bank it out of the terminus and remain with it as far as Clapham Junction via Longhedge. Having uncoupled at the junction station, the diesel then followed the steam train down to Portsmouth about 5 minutes behind, to render any assistance if required.

The route taken was via Barnes, Feltham, Virginia Water and Byfleet, where the main line was regained, thence down to Portsmouth via the Direct Line through Guildford and Haslemere, where a stop for water was made. It then continued via Havant, terminating at Portsmouth & Southsea High Level at 18.12, which was approached using the wrong (up) line.

Clan Line was displaying two white discs, one plain and the other marked 'SPL 1' (to denote a special train) on its buffer-beam. In Southern days the locomotive of such a train travelling over a non-scheduled route would almost certainly have carried one of the special three-disc head-codes. In addition it bore a headboard, rectangular and green, lettered 'RONALD G. JARVIS 1911-1994' and also a small wreath, in honour of the former Mechanical Engineer who had died on 2 September. Mr Jarvis had spent his career mainly on the London Midland Region from 1928 to 1950, before being transferred to the Southern Region, based at Brighton as Chief Technical Assistant to the Chief Mechanical Engineer (then Mr Oliver V. S. Bulleid) and in overall charge of the Southern's three drawing offices. Subsequently he was largely responsible for the redesign of the Bulleid 'Pacifics', and was also involved in design work on the BR Standard Class '4' and Class '9' locomotives.

On arrival at the High Level, No 47770 was coupled on to the rear of the train and drew the whole cavalcade to the electric multiple unit depot sidings at Fratton for servicing, including watering and coaling of the steam locomotive. It was necessary to turn the locomotive for the return journey, a process that, in former times, would have been effected at Fratton, but now had to be done using the triangle of lines north of Portsmouth. As the former crossovers at both Cosham station and the now demolished Farlington had been taken out (in fact a crossover still exists some 100 yards west of Cosham station, but it was not used, as it was learned that it would need to be operated manually), *Clan Line* needed to run 'light' from Fratton, tender-first to Fareham, thence to Havant chimney first and back to Fratton tender-first; this whole operation was performed between 19.43 and 20.44.

Once the carriages were shunted back to Portsmouth & Southsea station, the train departed for London

(Victoria) by the same route at 22.40, arriving at 00.50 with No 47770 again as back-up.

A week later the main run was carried out to identical timings, but this time *Clan Line* was in charge of a train of ten preserved Pullman carriages of the Venice-Simplon Orient Express plus two support coaches, and with Class 47 diesel No 47745 in red livery as back-up. As already mentioned, this was a fund-raising venture - on behalf of the Royal London Society for the Blind - and the headboard, worded 'RLSB ORIENT EXPRESS', was unveiled at Victoria by actress Jenny Seagrove prior to her performance in a West End show - she was reluctant to leave! Also, prior to departure, new nameplates on the diesel, carrying the Society name in both normal lettering and in Braille, were unveiled by actor Brian Blessed. Again two white discs were displayed on the steam locomotive's buffer-beam, both inscribed with a Society logo.

Tickets for the round trip cost £175, which included champagne and canapés in the Pullmans and dinner on board the former HMS *Warrior*, the preserved and restored 1860 battleship now moored adjacent to Portsmouth Dockyard. Many of the 200 passengers were in evening dress, and quite a number of steam railway enthusiasts had dipped into their pockets for their chance to travel on the Orient Express. Television personality Alan Whicker was one of the passengers on the train; he had returned time and again since the inaugural run in

1982, describing the Orient Express as 'exotic and glamorous'. The cost of tickets for the 'dry run' on the 17th was rather less, and it is understood that the passengers on that occasion were guests of BR and the charity and their friends. On both runs, tremendous public interest was aroused and huge numbers turned out to witness a nostalgic and memorable return of steam to the city, after an absence of 27 years. Both events were prominently reported in Portsmouth's local newspaper *THE NEWS*, which, incidentally, reported No 35028 *Clan Lane* as having been 'built by the Merchant Navy'!

So, after a lapse of 27 years, steam had returned to grace Portsmouth in some glory and with much public appreciation within the city and its boundaries. The small children standing on the footbridge at Fratton station stared in amazement - it was for many of them probably the very first time that they had seen a *real* steam engine.

Once the 'ice was broken', steam-hauled trains, mostly of an 'Orient Express' nature, have become a regular feature of the local scene, although the risk of fires being caused in the summer months, by stray sparks from the engine, frustratingly often leads to cancellation of advertised steam-hauled trains, with a diesel locomotive sometimes being substituted.

The authors wish to acknowledge the help and detail provided by Tom H. J. Dethridge in completing this text.

On Saturday 24 September 1994 the people of Portsmouth witnessed a nostalgic and memorable return of steam to the city after an absence of 27 years. Rebuilt 'Merchant Navy' Class 4-6-2 No

35028 *Clan Line* is seen near Somers Road Bridge with the renowned Orient Express, a ten-carriage Pullman train from London (Victoria) to Portsmouth & Southsea High Level. *Stuart Egbeare*

Above The view on Saturday 1 April 1995 from platform 3 of Fratton station. The Eastleigh Railway Preservation Society's preserved Class 'S15' 4-6-0 No 828 (former BR No 30828) is coupled to 'King Arthur' 4-6-0 No 30777 *Sir Lamiel* as they prepare to reverse their carriages to Portsmouth & Southsea High Level to form a unique double-headed railway enthusiasts' special to London (Victoria). This was the first steam special run by Waterman Railways. An emergency back-up diesel was on hand, Class 47 No 47756, if needed. *Stuart Egbeare*

Below No 828 reverses its carriages under Fratton Bridge on Sunday 11 February 1996 forming the 09.35 enthusiasts' special train to Clapham Junction. This was the first steam-hauled passenger train to depart from Portsmouth Harbour station since 1967. The train travelled via Horsham and the Mid-Sussex line and returned via the Direct Line (Godalming) before terminating at Fratton. Class 47 No 47701 then took the carriages to Portsmouth Harbour station. *Stuart Egbeare*

Above 'The Salisbury Flyer' steam special hauled by Class 'S15' 4-6-0 No 828 approaches Cosham on its return to Salisbury from Littlehampton on Sunday 21 May 1995. *Bruce Oliver*

Below Rebuilt 'West Country' Class 4-6-2 No 34027 *Taw Valley* draws its train of VSOE Pullmans slowly over Portcreek on a Sunday special from London (Victoria). At the time of writing this was its most recent visit, on Sunday 2 March 1997, having earlier performed similar duties in both January and February. No 35028 *Clan Line* featured on the same diagram during the autumn of 1996. It is of note that on this occasion the steam train was hard upon the heels of the preceding semi-fast service '82' from London (Waterloo). The attendant diesel locomotive, following No 34027 from London, was No 47784 *Condover Hall*, repeating a duty that had become very much its own preserve during this period of operation. *Bruce Oliver*

10.
THE FUTURE -
AND OPPORTUNITIES LOST?

As we head towards the Millennium, Hampshire County Council is well advanced in its plans for Phase 1 of a Light Rapid Transit System for the Fareham, Gosport and Portsmouth areas. The planned route of approximately 9 miles is intended to relieve the congestion on roads such as the A32 (Fareham to Gosport) and M27 (Fareham to Portsmouth), which are heavily used on account of the lack of a road link between Gosport and Portsmouth.

The route

The favoured route would start in Fareham shopping centre, then head towards the railway station, where interchange facilities would be provided. It would then follow

the route of the disused Fareham to Gosport railway line to the area of the former station at Gosport, and from here two route options are available before Portsmouth Harbour is reached. An 'immersed tube' tunnel will be constructed to link Gosport and Portsmouth for the first time. Phase 1 of the route will terminate in the pedestrianised shopping area of Commercial Road, but once again there is an optional route being considered that would take in the Gunwharf site and the Guildhall area prior to reaching Commercial Road.

Phase 1 by 2002

The initial 9-mile route would have 16 stops and a total journey time of around half an hour. In 1995 capital costs were estimated at £121 million, and it is hoped, subject to Department of Transport approval and finance being available, to have Phase 1 operational by the year 2002. In the longer term, further phases would, hopefully, link Cosham, Havant and Waterlooville, and possibly, even further in the future, Southampton.

Driving out the car

Faced with an ever-increasing number of vehicles in south-east Hampshire, the County Council is dedicated to driving the car away from busy areas and is already significantly reducing the sizes of roads by cutting the number of available traf-

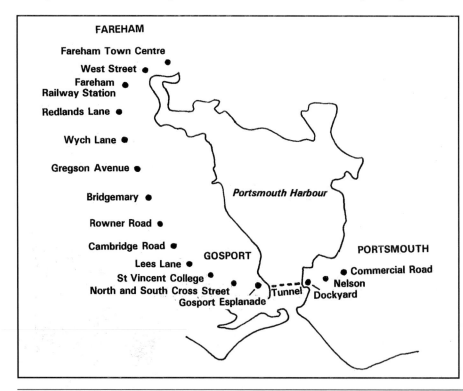

The route of the Light Rapid Transit System proposed for the Portsmouth, Gosport and Fareham areas, as at December 1996.

fic lanes and providing dedicated routes for pedal cyclists, which, regrettably, seem totally out of proportion to the current perceived needs of cyclists, a large proportion of whom seem to prefer cycling on pavements anyway! In addition, 'Park and Ride' schemes seem to be becoming increasingly popular, while buses are given priority over cars on certain routes.

How it could have been

Hopefully, the Light Rapid Transit System will provide a sensible, cost-effective alternative for today's increasingly frustrated motorists. However, one cannot help contemplating whether, with a little forethought perhaps half a century ago, things could have been very different. Consider the situation then - Gosport, Portsmouth and Hayling Island all had separate branches off the cross-country rail route from Fareham, through Cosham, to Havant. A shuttle service linking the six areas would surely have been viable, more so today, bearing in mind the increased population and the industrial sites that have been established on the edges of urban areas. Such a service would, no doubt, have ensured the continuation of railway travel on the Gosport and Hayling Island branches.

A final thought. . .

As a final thought, our Victorian ancestors were known to be keen to provide a railway link between Portsmouth and Hayling Island. Had this been done, the next logical step would have been a bridge across Portsmouth Harbour to link with Gosport. This, in turn, could have provided a double circle of routes, encompassing the whole area, and this could have been operated today at frequent intervals by modern electric multiple units, thereby removing the need for the provision of the Rapid Transit System now planned. The very nature of the Hayling Island branch line could have permitted the operation of steam locomotives at weekends as a summer attraction for holidaymakers . . . what a dream!

Local societies

If you have enjoyed reading this book and would like more information about the railway history of the Portsmouth area, there are several railway societies that meet regularly.

They all welcome visitors or new members, and their programmes normally consist of film or slide shows, historical talks, outings, etc. Those in the area are:

The Mid-Hants Railway Preservation Society (Portsmouth Group): Tel 01705 383872

The Gosport Railway Society: Tel 01705 582499

The Meon Valley Locomotive Society: Tel 01489 894051

INDEX OF LOCATIONS

Page numbers in *italics* refer to illustrations.

Albert Road Halt 81, *81*
Aldershot 82
Alfred Road, Dockyard branch 47, 54
Alton 60, 82-3, 101

Basingstoke 76, 82, 101, 122
Bedenham 43, 47, 48, 52, 61
Bedhampton 24, 43, 47, 52, 92, *109-10*
Big Whale Island 50
Bishopstoke 60
Bishops Waltham 60, 67, 68-9, 69, 78
Blackfriars Junction 97
Blockhouse Fort/Lake 91
Botley 60, 67, *67*, 69
Bournemouth 76, 78, 94-6, 101
Bransbury Park Railway 89, *90*, 91
Bridgemary 91
Brighton 8-10, 27, 94-7, 101
Bristol 8, 98, 101
Browndown 66
Buriton Tunnel 11, 111, *114-7*
Bursledon 67

Cardiff 77, 98
Chichester 7-8
City of Portsmouth Preserved Transport Depot 91, *91*
Clarence Pier 80
Cosham 7-8, 9, 11, *19-21*, *32*, 59, 89, 91-2, 101, *119-20*, 122, *125*, 126-7

Denvilles 10
Dockyard, Royal Naval 8, 43, *45*, 46, *47*, 50, 54, 123
Dorking 7, 10
Droxford 67, 78, 83, 85, 87
Durley Halt 67

East Hayling Light Railway 88, 88
Eastleigh 7, 9, 27, 31, 60, 67, 76, 78, 101, 122
Eastney Pumping Station 91
East Southsea 11
Edinburgh Road, Dockyard branch 8, 47, *49*, 54
Elmore 66
Excellent, HMS 43, 50, *50*

Fareham 7-9, 11, *22-23*, 60-1, *61*, 82-3, 82, 122, 126-7
Farlington 11, 91, 101, *107-8*, 122
Fort Brockhurst 60, 66
Fort Gomer Halt 66
Fountain Lake 50, *50*
Frater 43, 52
Fratton 11, *15*, *16-18*, 26-8, 31, *42*, 47, 52, 54, *55-57*, 71, 78, 80-1, 98, 101, *102-4*, 122-3, *124*
  Locomotive Depot *26-42*, 55
Fratton East 26

Gilkicker 91
Godalming 8-9, 82
Goodwillie, J. F. Ltd 92
Gosport 7, 43, 52, 60-1, *63-4*, 65, 76, 83, 92, 126-7
Gosport Road 65
Green Lanes Crossing *19*
Guildford 8-9, 26-7, 76, 94, 96, 122
Gunwharf 43, 126

Haslar Tramway/Marina 91
Haslemere 9, 60, 111, 122
Havant 8-11, *25*, 70-1, *72-3*, *75*, 77, 97, *112-3*, 126-7
Hayling Island 10-11, 67, 70-1, *71*, *74*, 76, *79*, 92, 122, 127
Hilsea 8-9, *57-8*, 106, *107*; Gas Works *19*, 91, *105*; Lido 89
Hilsea Miniature Railway 89, *90*

Horsea Island 92

Idsworth *116*
Isle of Wight 10, 54, 60-1, 65, 76, 78, 80, 82

'Jacob's Ladder' footbridge 26
Jessie Road Halt 81
John Pound's Scrapyard, Tipner 92

Knowle 78, 83, *83*, *121*

Landport 8
Langstone 10, 70, *73*, 76, *77*, *79*
Lee-on-the-Solent 61, 66, *66*
Little Anglesey viaduct 65
Little Whale Island 50
London 7, 9, 51, 60-1, 77, 101, 122
  Victoria 94, 122
  Waterloo 65, 76, 83, 94-5, 101

Meon Valley 60-1, 67, 78, 82-3
Mid-Hants Railway 47, 77
Midhurst 8, 83
Mislingford 83, 85
Monckton 91

Netley 31, 60, 76
Nine Elms 60, 76
North Hayling 70, *74*, 76

Old Portsmouth 8, 91

Paulsgrove 11, 92
Petersfield 9, 82, 111, *118-9*
Portchester 11, 92, *121*
Portcreek 8, 10, 11, *106-7*, *125*
Portsea Island 8, 11, 43, 61
Portsmouth & Southsea 11, *13*, *14*, *15*, 46, 49, 53, 54, 55, 97, 99, *100*, *101*, 122, *123*
Portsmouth City Airport 91

Portsmouth Guildhall 54, 126
Portsmouth Harbour *1*, 7, 10-11, *11*, *12*, 43, 46, 52, 60, 65, 80, 95, 98, 126-7
Port Solent 92
Priddy's Hard 43, 52
Privett 66, 82, 87
Pycroft's brickfield 92

Ropley *33*, 67, 82
Rowlands Castle 11, 111, *114*
Royal Clarence Yard 43, 60
Ryde 65, 76

Salisbury 76-7, 98
Southall Railway Centre 92, *92*, 122
Southampton 7-8, 60, 76-7, 82, 97-8, 101; Docks 27, 78
South Hayling 70-1
South Railway Jetty 46
Southsea 10, 80-2, *81*
Southsea Miniature Railway 89, 89
Stockheath Crossing *111*
Stokes Bay 61, 65, *65*, 80
Stokes Bay Miniature Railway 91
Sullivan's 92, *93*

Tisted 87

Unicorn Gate, Dockyard branch 8, 47, *48*, *49*

Vernon, HMS 76
Victoria Park 43, 54
Victualling Yard 60, 92

Watering Island line 43, 46, 47
West Leigh 11
West Meon 82-3, 86
Whale Island 43, 50, *50*
Wickham 83, 85
Winchester 67, 82, 97, 101
Workhouse viaduct 65